The Pure in Heart

The Historical Development of The Baha'i Faith in China, Southeast Asia and Far East

By Jimmy Ewe Huat Seow

BAHA'I PUBLICATIONS AUSTRALIA

Published by
Baha'i Publications Australia
PO Box 285, Mona Vale, NSW 2103
© Copyright Mr Jimmy Seow 1991
All Copyrights reserved

ISBN 0 909991 41 3

Typeset in Baskerville

Phototypesetting and Colour Separations by:
Photoset Computer Service
Sydney, NSW

Dedicated to Uncle Yan Kee Leong,
the first enlightened believer of Malaysia,
my wife Mona and daughter Layli.

The Baha'i Faith upholds the unity of God, recognises the unity of His Prophets, and inculcates the principle of the oneness and wholeness of the entire human race. It proclaims the necessity and the inevitability of the unification of mankind, asserts that it is gradually approaching, and claims that nothing short of the transmuting spirit of God, working through His chosen Mouthpiece in this day, can ultimately succeed in bringing it about. It, moreover, enjoins upon its followers the primary duty of an unfettered search after truth, condemns all manner of prejudice and superstition, declares the purpose of religion to be the promotion of amity and concord, proclaims its essential harmony with science, and recognises it as the foremost agency for the pacification and the orderly progress of human society. It unequivocally maintains the principle of equal rights, opportunities and privileges for men and women, insists on compulsory education, eliminates extremes of poverty and wealth, abolishes the institution of priesthood, prohibits slavery, asceticism, mendicancy and monasticism, prescribes monogamy, discourages divorce, emphasises the necessity of strict obedience to one's government, exalts any work performed in the spirit of service to the level of worship, urges either the creation or the selection of an auxiliary international language, and delineates the outlines of those institutions that must establish and perpetuate the general peace of mankind.

Shoghi Effendi.

Contents

Illustrations

'Abdu'l-Baha in Adrianople.

'Akka, the Most Great Prison.

Jamal Effendi, Conqueror of India.

Siyyid Mustafa Rumi, builder of the Burmese Baha'i community.

A group of Baha'is in China *circa* 1930.

Dr. Sun Yat-sen, the Father of the Republic of China.

Martha Root and Agnes Alexander in Japan *circa* 1915.

Martha Root in Shanghai, 1 July 1937.

Newspaper articles written by Martha Root in China and Hong Kong.

Baha'is of China *circa* 1931.

Hand of the Cause of God, Keith Ransom-Kehler.

Chinese aviators in Colorado, United States of America.

Chan S. Liu, an early Chinese Baha'i.

Dr. Zia Bagdadi.

An early Chinese Baha'i family.

John E. Esslemont, author of *Baha'u'llah and the New Era.*

Hilda Yank Sing <u>Yen.</u>

Hilda Yen as a member of the Baha'i Delegation to the United Nations International Conference of Non-Governmental Organizations in 1949.

Siegfried Schopflocher, Hand of the Cause of God.

M. Hippolyte Dreyfus-Barney.

Bernard Leach, famous Baha'i potter.

Mark Tobey, famous Baha'i painter.

'Abdu'l-Baha and Shoghi Effendi.

Hand of the Cause of God Dr. Rahmatu'llah Muhajir, in Penang, Malaysia.

Martha Root with Dr. K.M. and Shirin Fozdar in India.

Yan Kee Leong with the first two Chinese believers of Burma.

Hand of the Cause of God Dr. Rahmatu'llah Muhajir.

Mr. Hushmand Fatheazam, member of the Universal House of Justice, addressing a large gathering of Chinese Baha'i believers and enquirers in Malaysia, 1965.

Leong Tat Chee, famous Malaysian Chinese Baha'i believer.

First Spiritual Assembly of the Baha'is of Singapore, 1952.

First Spiritual Assembly of the Baha'is of Kuching, Sarawak, East Malaysia, 1953.

First Spiritual Assembly of the Baha'is of Victoria, Hong Kong, 1956.

First Spiritual Assembly of the Baha'is of Brunei Town, Brunei, 1957.

First Spiritual Assembly of the Baha'is of Taipei, Taiwan, 1958.

First Spiritual Assembly of the Baha'is of Phnom Penh, Cambodia, April 1959.

Carl A. and Loretta L. Scherer, Knights of Baha'u'llah for Macau.

Baha'is of Macau, 1955.

The first National Spiritual Assembly of the Baha'is of Malaysia, Ridvan 1964.

The first National Spiritual Assembly of the Baha'is of Brunei, Ridvan 1966.

The first National Spiritual Assembly of the Baha'is of Taiwan, Ridvan 1967.

The first National Spiritual Assembly of the Baha'is of Hong Kong, Ridvan 1974.

The first National Spiritual Assembly of the Baha'is of Singapore, Ridvan 1972.

Forward

The expansion of the Baha'i Faith throughout the world during the past century has been truly remarkable. In less than one hundred years our Faith has been established in more countries of the globe than any other religion except Christianity. Yet, because of circumstances inherent in the political structure of the Communist countries, the peoples of eastern Europe and the USSR were deprived of easy access to the Baha'i teachings. These populations taken together with the over one billion people in China account for approximately two-fifths of the world's population.

In the late 1980s the collapse of Communist doctrines in eastern Europe and the USSR made possible the introduction of free religious practices. In 1989 and 1990 great strides were made in the Baha'i teaching work in those countries and Local Assemblies were established in such places as Ashkhabad, Budapest, Moscow, Kiev and Bucharest. These people, having been deprived of religion for many decades, were found to be thirsting for spiritual values that would give a fuller meaning to life.

China, however, is exceedingly ambivalent on the question of religion. On the one hand it is said that China has freedom of religion; at the same time its actual practice is surrounded by uncertainty. While we can be sure that the social and economic principles proclaimed by Baha'u'llah[1] are what China needs and the Chinese are searching for, we must be very careful not to offend Chinese sensibilities, nor to compromise those Chinese who believe in Baha'u'llah.

---

1   Prophet-Founder of the Baha'i Faith and Manifestation of God for this Day. He was born Mirza Husayn-'Ali in Mazindaran, Iran, on 12 November 1817. Passed away in the Mansion of Bahji in Palestine (now Israel) at the age of seventy-four on 29 May 1892. Revealed numerous Tablets and Writings in both Persian and Arabic concerning religious revelations, ethical and moral questions, government, education, environment, metaphysical matters, social, economic and scientific matters, etc.

Nevertheless the Chinese are entitled to know the principles by which we live our lives, and it is our purpose to inform the Chinese of our beliefs wherever and whenever it is possible to do so without violating any law or placing them in jeopardy. There are already substantial Baha'i communities in Taiwan, Hong Kong, Macau, Singapore and Malaysia. Recently, renewed emphasis has been placed on reaching the members of this noble race residing in other places outside the mainland. To assist in this process, Mr. Seow has drawn together in this monograph some of the salient facts about the history of the Faith in China. It is hoped that this effort will be a source of inspiration and guidance for those who wish to teach the Chinese wherever they may be.

Hugh E. Chance[2]
Haifa
September 1990

---

2 Member of the Universal House of Justice

Preface

The idea of writing a paper on the early history of Chinese teaching[3] arose in early 1989 when I had the opportunity to present a talk on the subject at the second Chinese Teaching Conference in Perth, Western Australia, held in July of that year. The talk was presented together with a series of slides of the early Chinese believers and Baha'is who were involved in Chinese teaching in China, Southeast Asia and the Far East. The talk was re-written and presented as a paper at the subsequent National Conference of the Association for Baha'i Studies of Australia, held in April 1990 at Murdoch University, Perth, Western Australia. The idea of publishing the paper and its accompanying photographs as a separate publication was put forward after the Conference by that Association. The prime purpose of publishing this paper is to stimulate interest in Chinese teaching in light of its importance and expansion throughout the world. It is also important to record the early history of the Baha'i Faith. I am particularly inspired in this regard by the advice of Hand of the Cause of God Mr. A.Q. Faizi to Mr. O.Z. Whitehead: *"Write down every Baha'i experience that you have. Before long people will want to know about Baha'is, no matter how obscure they may be. One line that anyone writes could be very important[4]."*

This paper is an attempt to present to the reader an impression of the lives and events of the early Baha'i pioneers and Chinese believers who had the self-sacrifice and courage to travel to such remote and, at times, dangerous places for the promotion of the Baha'i Faith. Present information is limited, so detailed backgrounds of some people and events are brief. Another objective of the paper is to provide some background information for the purpose of Chinese teaching.

The author intends to expand this publication and welcomes any information or photographs readers may have. Please forward them to 28 Robertson Place, Bibra Lake, Perth, Western Australia 6163 Tel: 09-4175762.

---

3   Common Baha'i term for teaching the Baha'i Faith to the Chinese people. Baha'is are not permitted to proselytise.

4   O.Z. Whitehead. *Some Early Baha'is Of The West.* George Ronald, Oxford, 1976, p.ix.

Acknowledgment

I am grateful to the Baha'i World Centre for providing me with a copy of notes on the Chronology of Baha'is in China when my wife and I were on pilgrimage in the Holy Land in 1986. That information provided the foundation for this paper. Many of the details concerning Martha Root were taken from both the informative book by M.R. Garis, *Martha Root: Lioness at the Threshold*, and *The Baha'i World* volumes.

I would like to thank the Association for Baha'i Studies of Australia for providing me with the opportunity of publishing this paper, the Research Department of the Universal House of Justice[5] for providing me with some of the research materials and photographs of the early Chinese believers, my wife Mona for her encouragement and assistance and her suggestion to name the paper 'The Pure in Heart', and Mr. Anthony Temple for his assistance in the production of the photographs. I am especially indebted to Mr. Michael Day for editing the manuscript and providing many useful comments. I am also appreciative of the comments received from Counsellor Dr. John Fozdar, the Baha'i International Community Committee for China, the National Spiritual Assembly of the Baha'is of Malaysia, the National Spiritual Assembly of the Baha'is of Hong Kong, the International Chinese Teaching Committee and Dr. Graham Hassall.

Also the contribution of Miss Natalie Louch for providing information on the first Chinese 'believer' of Indonesia and Mr. Kit Yin-Kiang for providing the names of the members of the first NSA of Taiwan.

---

5   Supreme administrative body of the Baha'i Faith ordained by Baha'u'llah in the *Kitab-i-Aqdas*. The Seat of the Universal House of Justice is located on Mount Carmel, Haifa, Israel.

Introduction

History forms an important and integral part of our lives, and can provide us with insight for the future. As such, the history of the early Baha'i believers who were instrumental in the promulgation of the Baha'i Faith in China, Southeast Asia and the Far East, is important for the present generation of believers as it can inspire and encourage them further in their teaching work. The development of Chinese teaching and the evolution of the Baha'i community in those regions need to be understood in order that the Baha'i community may obtain fresh ideas and a broader perspective for the future. Looking to the past to help obtain a vision of the future provides Baha'is with new direction in the establishment of the New World Order of Baha'u'llah in those regions.

The task ahead can be daunting because of the sheer number of people Baha'is have to reach but they are assured in the Baha'i Writings that there will be manifold victories and assistance should they arise to serve. The spiritualization of the Chinese people is certainly an important element in the unfolding process of the maturation of mankind. 'Abdu'l-Baha[6] proclaimed: *"China is the country of the future"*. He hoped that *"the right kind of teacher will be inspired to go to that vast empire to lay the foundation of the Kingdom of God, to promote the principles of divine civilization, to unfurl the banner of the Cause of Baha'u'llah, and to invite the people to the banquet of the Lord!"*[7].

History was created by the early Baha'is, and now the present generation of Baha'i believers themselves have the opportunity to provide inspiration for future generations should they enter the field of service to which they are called. Shoghi Effendi[8], the Guardian[9] of the Baha'i Faith, encouraged "... *the friends*

---

6   23 May 1844 — 28 November 1921. Eldest son of Baha'u'llah. Appointed by Baha'u'llah as His Successor and Interpreter of His Writings. Given the titles of Ghusn-i-A'zam (the Most Great Branch), Sirru'llah (Mystery of God) and Aqa (the Master) by Baha'u'llah. He began His travels to Europe and North America to proclaim His Father's message in 1911. Knighted by the British government in 1920 for his service and efforts in relieving hunger in Palestine during the First World War.

7   *Star of the West, Vol. 13.* George Ronald, Oxford, 1984, pp.185-186.

8   Appointed by 'Abdu'l-Baha in His *Will and Testament* as the 'guardian of the Cause of God' and 'the expounder of the words of God'. Succeeded 'Abdu'l-Baha after His passing in 1921. Shoghi Effendi was the eldest grandson of 'Abdu'l-Baha and was born on 1 March 1897 in Akka. He passed away on 4 November 1957 in London.

9   The Institution of Guardianship was created by 'Abdu'l-Baha in His Will and Testament for the function of authoritative interpretation of the Baha'i Sacred Writings and the care and protection of the Baha'i Faith.

in the East and in the West to both enter the field. Let them awaken and quicken the land of China — a land which has its own world and civilization, whose people constitute one-fourth of the population of the globe, which ranks foremost among all nations in the material, cultural and spiritual resources and potentialities, and whose future is assuredly bright. Let them draw that vast and mighty land under the shadow of the Word of God, cause its peoples to associate with the other nations of the world, and demonstrate the true oneness of mankind, which can alone be established through the power of Baha'u'llah [10]".

The social, political and economic environment of China, Southeast Asia and the Far East towards the end of the nineteenth century and in the early half of the twentieth century was one of uncertainty and transition. New ideas and thinking pertaining to new forms of government and political systems, reformation of the existing social order, and restructuring of the economy were taking place in the region. In China numerous reform movements were initiated by various reformers, writers, intellectuals and poets. Prominent among them was Kang Youwei (1858-1927), who in 1902 published one of his many interesting works, the *Datongshu* [11] *(The Book of the Great Togetherness)*, an eclectic and utopian work advocating the reformation of the fast collapsing traditional Chinese society. In the *Datongshu,* Kang strongly advocated the philosophy of the brotherhood of man and unity of nations as one which the Chinese must adopt in order to end class distinctions and social disorder caused by slavery, caste systems, or the remnants of aristocratic and feudal institutions. Kang's ideas were taken up by other writers and thinkers and had great influence upon the Chinese intelligentsia of that period as they were searching for new ideas and inspiration to meet the needs of modern China. But the Chinese revolutionary intellectuals to have greatest impact upon both Chinese thinking and the reform movement in the early twentieth century, were scholar and writer Chen Duxiu (1879-1942) and Li Dazhao (1889-1927), the principal co-founders of the Chinese Communist party. Chen and Li believed that China needed to wholly implement the guiding principles of Marxism-Leninism in order for her to be modernised and to regain her former status as a great and mighty country. Their newly adopted socio-political ideas eventually changed the political system of China.

Towards the end of the nineteenth century in China, the Qing Dynasty was in the twilight of its reign due to internal squabbles of the officials, short-sightedness of its policy-makers, and feuding between the various factions of the

---

10   Shoghi Effendi, letter to the Baha'is of the East dated 23 January 1923.
11   Completed in Darjeeling, India, in 1902.

administration. China was fast becoming outdated especially in comparison to the technologically developed western countries. It became a Republic on 12 February 1912 with the abdication of its last Qing Emperor, Puyi, ending two hundred and sixty eight years of imposed Manchurian rule. The most familiar symbol of that rule was the compulsory wearing by men of a queue (a long pigtail of hair).

In the 1830s the British actively exported opium to China as a countermeasure to alter their trade imbalance. The Chinese authorities, incensed by the growing addiction of its people to this newly introduced drug, seized several chests of opium in Canton which resulted in the First Opium War[12]. The British naval forces easily defeated the Qing authorities because they were far superior technologically. The defeat resulted in the signing of the Ch'uan-pi Convention on 20 January 1841, which provided for the cession of Hong Kong, payment of a large indemnity, recognition of 'equality' in official Sino-British negotiations, and full resumption of trade. Several later wars were fought between the Chinese authorities and the British forces, resulting in further defeat of the Qing authorities and the signing of other treaties. The Treaty of Nanking in 1842 gave Britain further trade concessions, an indemnity, access to five additional ports for trade (Canton, Amoy, Foochow, Ningpo and Shanghai), and cession of a larger area of Hong Kong. China, greatly weakened by those ensuing wars agreed to demands for trade concessions by other foreign powers such as Russia, Germany, France, the United States of America and Japan. The Treaty of Nanking, the first of the unequal treaties to be imposed on China, had far-reaching consequences as it led to a century of degradation and ignominious humiliation, which has been bitterly resented by the Chinese to the present day. As a result of those events, several groups and individuals arose to put forward their ideas for political and social reform. Many sought to strengthen the weakened Qing Dynasty to enable it to contain further foreign domination and imperialism. Others wanted to unite the nation against the foreign aggressors. Some wanted to entirely replace the corrupt Qing administration with a new and modern political structure and establishment. The ensuing confrontation between those opposing political ideologies was to bring much chaos, disorder and civil war in China for the greater part of the late nineteenth and early twentieth century. China came under Communist rule when the Chinese Communist Party defeated the Kuomintang (Guomindang) National Party[13] on 1 October 1949.

---

12   Started on 3 November 1839.
13   Formed in 1912 with a stated objective of endowing the new Republic of China with an appropriate constitutional and parliamentary structure. Its most prominent leader was Chiang Kai-shek.

The other countries in the region did not suffer such drastic events as China but nevertheless they too were in turmoil because they were fighting for freedom and independence from their colonial rulers. The war years from 1937 to 1945, when Japan invaded its neighbouring countries, brought further suffering, hardship and chaos to the region.

In the same period, many of the Southeast Asian countries were European colonies or under European domination. Malaya (now West Malaysia), Singapore, Burma and parts of Borneo (now Sabah, Sarawak and Brunei) were under British colonial rule and formed part of the British Empire. Indo-China (now Vietnam, Laos and Cambodia) was under French rule. A large part of the Indonesian archipelago (e.g. Java, Sumatra) was occupied and administered by the Dutch, with other islands being colonised by the Portuguese (e.g. Portuguese Timor). Most of those countries only gained independence in the late 1940s and 1950s.

One of the most interesting features of Chinese society is the peoples' religious belief and practice, which varies in different places. To define what constitutes a 'Chinese religion' is very difficult and to say that the Chinese do not possess a 'true religion' would do injustice to their religious beliefs and convictions. The Chinese 'religion' is really one of amalgamation and synthesis due to various influences through centuries of animism, Buddhism, Confucianism[14] and Taoism[15].

Buddhism was introduced to China in the first century A.D. but did not take firm root until the third century. It achieved its first success in northern China and by 500 A.D. most of the population had been converted. By the seventh century (period of the Tang Dynasty 681-907 A.D.), Buddhism had become a

---

14   Confucius (551-479 B.C.) is China's first known educator. His ideas, now known as Confucianism (a European term), are devoid of metaphysical or religious speculation and are drawn from the earlier Chou era (1122?-256 B.C.). The Golden Age advocated by Confucius must follow a set way — the Tao - whereby people must conform to their proper place in society and observe all customary rites. This self-disciplinary philosophy can only be achieved through education and adherence to proper moral and ethical principles. The transformation of Confucianism into a state ideology occurred much later with much distortion. Confucianism had great impact upon Chinese government bureaucracy and political ideology and Chinese social order.

15   Lao Tzu (6th century), the founder of Taoism and author of *Tao te ching* ('The Way and the Power'). It is a philosophy of withdrawal or going back to nature as a protest against the evils of society and has the guiding principle of 'wu wei', meaning 'doing what is natural'. Taoist contemplation of nature led to early Chinese sciences. Taoism was later transformed by Buddhist influence into a popular religion and it borrowed many of its rituals and religious paraphernalia from Buddhism. Taoist temples were modelled on Buddhist temples.

powerful economic force within China but its political influence was still limited. Rodzinski[16] (1984) states that: *"the rise of Buddhism had by no means signified the total elimination of opposing creeds ... the continued presence and influence of Taoism and Confucianism also prevented the Buddhist church from attaining complete domination, while the coexistence of the three creeds probably helped to mould the noteworthy non-absolutist and eclectic approach of the Chinese to religious matters."* With time, Buddhism became sinified to the point where it lost much of its original form. Buddhism was successful in China due to its general tolerant approach and was therefore capable of assimilating concepts from rival creeds such as Taoism and Confucianism. It had great influence on Chinese society up to the nineteenth century. Buddhist influence upon Chinese art and literature was immense, especially in the Tang period.

The form of Buddhism practised in China was the Mahayana, a creed quite distinct from the original ethical teaching of Buddha[17]. It was much like a new religion in itself, and was richly endowed with rituals and a huge pantheon of Buddhas and Bodhisattvas[18], at the same time intermingled with various forms of metaphysical philosophy.

Buddhism was first brought to Southeast Asia in the first century A.D. by Indian merchants who traded and settled in port cities in the region. Some of the early kingdoms such as Srivijaya[19] adopted Buddhism as a state religion. Theravada (Hinayana) Buddhism, one of the two major creeds of Buddhism, was brought from Ceylon (Sri Lanka) by traders in the sixth century. It was later replaced by the other creed of Buddhism, Mahayana Buddhism, which is a more 'democratic' form of the religion. Hinayana Buddhism is a nontheistic school of Buddhism, which emphasised the 'Way of living' as taught by Buddha and has a monastic tradition. On the other hand, Mahayana Buddhism, other than following the Way of Buddha, emphasized that every devout believer has the potential of achieving the station of Buddha.

Hinduism in China was almost non-existent. That religion, like Buddhism, was brought to Southeast Asia by Indian merchants, who were also instrumental in contributing Indian culture to the historical development of

---

16   Witold Rodzinski. *The Walled Kingdom: A History of China from 2000 BC to the Present.* Fontana Paperbacks, London, 1984, p.81.

17   Born Siddhartha Gautama, a Messenger of God and founder of Buddhism, who appeared about 560 B.C. Buddha means 'The Illumined One'.

18   Images of Buddha.

19   Early Sumatran maritime empire which dominated trade throughout Southeast Asia and between India and China during the 7th to 13th century.

Southeast Asia. It was easily adopted by the rulers of the region such as the Majapahit[20], Mataram[21] kingdoms in Indonesia and the Khmer[22] kingdom in Indo-China (Cambodia). Those kingdoms largely modelled their ways of government practice and court ceremonies upon Hindu ideas and practices, and followed Hindu ideas in their religion. The Mataram kingdom later adopted Mahayana Buddhism as it was more progressive. It built many magnificent Buddhist monuments such as the famous Borobodur temple. Hence a large part of Southeast Asia was under the influence of Hinduism or had Hindu rulers at various periods of its history. Those dominant Hindu influences are still clearly discernible today in many local cultures of the Buddhist countries in the region (Thailand, Burma and Indo-China). For example, various dances and puppet shows there are based on the *Ramayana*[23].

Christianity first reached China in the 16th century with the arrival of Portuguese colonisers and Jesuit missionaries. In 1583 Matteo Ricci (1557-1610), an Italian Jesuit, was the first Roman Catholic to arrive in China. The fundamental objective of the Jesuit missionaries was to convert the Chinese to Christianity but, unlike the case with Buddhism, mass acceptance of Christianity was not attained. The failure of the early Christians to convert the Chinese was due to a number of factors, such as persecution during the Qing Dynasty, acrimonious rivalry among the Catholic missionaries and, most significant of all, the growing disrepute brought upon the Christian faith by the activities of its purported believers and the European colonisers in East Asia. Foreign control of China after the Opium War allowed the Christian missionaries, both Catholic and Protestant, to spread their faith unhampered throughout the entire country. But due to their aggressive approach, arrogance and concealed contempt for Chinese custom and habits, innumerable conflicts both with the local and the Qing authorities occurred. Those anti-Christian feelings became intertwined with xenophobia, and both attitudes were further exacerbated by subsequent foreign exploitation and injustice heaped upon the Chinese. The most significant anti-foreign event was the Boxer Rebellion in Peking (now Beijing) in 1899.

In Southeast Asia, Christianity was also introduced by the European

---

20   Early Indonesian kingdom (13th-16th century) founded in Java.
21   Early Indonesian kingdom founded in central Java. The Kings were known as Sailendras.
22   9th-12th century Cambodian kingdom.
23   Hindu epic poem.

colonisers (mainly the Portuguese) and Jesuit missionaries[24] in the 16th century. The Spaniards brought the Catholic faith to the Philippine islands. When they arrived, they found that most local inhabitants were still animists[25], although some Hindu influences had penetrated from Java. In the south, Islam was already firmly established. The Portuguese were responsible for spreading Christianity to Malacca[26] (now part of West Malaysia), Borneo (now East Malaysia, Brunei and Indonesian Kalimantan), the Celebes (now Sulawesi), New Guinea (now Irian Jaya and Papua New Guinea), Timor and other islands of the Indonesian archipelago. However, their attempt to firmly establish Christianity had little success as by that time Islam was already widely accepted in the region. The European colonisers at times used force to convert the local population to accept their faith, and so their attempts to propagate Christianity in the region led to constant animosity with the local Muslim states. The Dutch brought Protestantism to the Dutch East Indies colonies (now Indonesia) and were often in conflict with the Roman Catholic missionaries. Animosity and rivalry between the European colonisers and missionaries, as in China, did not endear the local population to Christianity and were major reasons for Christianity not being firmly established in the region. Besides, Islam, considered a more modern and progressive region than Christianity, was more acceptable to both the local rulers and population. The French were mainly responsible for introducing the Catholic Faith to Indo-China[27] in the same period.

Islam had little impact on China except in the western border region. It was introduced mainly by Arab traders during the Tang Dynasty. On the other hand, Islam had a dominant influence in Southeast Asia. Arab traders and seamen first brought that faith to the region's port cities in the 7th century but it was not well established. Not until the 15th century did Islam become established and widely spread in the region. Gujerati Muslim traders from western India introduced Islam to north Sumatra from where it later spread to

---

24   St. Francis Xavier, a famous Portuguese missionary, arrived in Malacca in 1545 and went to
      the Spice Islands just before his death in 1552.
25   Believing in the spirit of nature.
26   City founded in 1402 by Parameswara, an exiled Sailendra Hindu prince who married a
      princess of the Majapahit Empire. Parameswara converted to Islam. He died in 1424. At the
      height of Malacca's power and fame, major communities of Chinese, Arabs, Indians,
      Indonesians and Persians were recorded as living there (Milton Osborne. *Southeast Asia: An
      Illustrated Introductory History.* Allen & Unwin, Sydney, 1988, p.103).
27   By the middle of 18th century it was reported that there were about 300,000 Roman Catholics
      in Cochin-China or Vietnam.

Malacca. By the end of the 15th century, many of the rulers of the port cities of Java had been converted to Islam and by the 18th century most of southern Thailand, the Malay peninsula and the Indonesian archipelago, with the exception of Bali, had large Muslim populations. Islam later replaced Hinduism as the state religion of the Majapahit kingdom but it was highly discouraged under the Dutch colonial rule and the Muslims were persecuted for their religious convictions. The revival of Islam in the Dutch East Indies, which occurred at the end the 19th century, was responsible to a large extent for the foundation of the rise of Indonesian nationalism in the 20th century.

Another important aspect of Chinese religious belief is the concept of the supernatural. Wolf (1974)[28], through his personal studies and other research done mainly in Hong Kong and Taiwan, notes the existence of three major categories of spiritual beings. They are gods ('cieng-sin'), ghosts ('kui') and ancestors ('kong-ma' or 'co-kong'). They are arranged in pairs of cross-cutting opposition. Gods are contrasted with ghosts and ancestors; ghosts are contrasted with gods and ancestors; and ancestors are contrasted with gods and ghosts. For example, gods are offered uncooked food (or whole) food while ghosts and ancestors are offered cooked food. Gods are considered to be the supernatural counterparts of the imperial bureaucracy and they reside in temples guarded by divine generals. They punish people for their crimes against society but they are also easily bribed (e.g. by an offer of food); they write reports, keep records, and are associated with different administrative districts. Ghosts are the supernatural counterparts of despised, dangerous strangers and are worshipped outside temples and at the back door of homes. They are considered dangerous and sometimes malicious. These ghosts are offered food and clothing that are thought of as handouts or payoffs, so are compared to bandits, beggars, and gangsters. Ancestors are senior members of one's own line of descent, the people to whom one is indebted for the material and spiritual benefits of this world. They have the right to be prayed for and worshipped and are offered food in the form of a meal.

Ancestral worship has been practised by the Chinese since the earliest recorded times. Inscribed bones used as oracles during the Shang Dynasty (1776-1122 B.C.) showed that the Chinese practised a form of ancestral worship (Baker, 1979)[29]. Chinese ancestral worship is a form of reciprocity in which the individuals exist by virtue of their descendants, and their ancestors exist only through them i.e. the spiritual well-being of the ancestors is dependant upon

---

28   Wolf, A.P. (Ed.). *Religion and Ritual In Chinese Society*. Stanford University Press, California, 1974.

29   Baker, H.D. *Chinese Family and Kinship*. MacMillan Press, London, 1979.

their descendants through their prayers and material sacrifice at altars; and the descendants are dependant upon their ancestors through their spiritual assistance and guidance.

Over the years the Chinese religious beliefs have evolved into popular cults, superstitions and general practice especially among the overseas Chinese. Large-scale immigration from China[30] to Southeast Asia occurred in the nineteenth century, with many of those newly arrived immigrants settling in cities or near commercial centres of the region. As a result, the various forms of Buddhism and Chinese religious beliefs of nineteenth century China were introduced to the host countries of the region. At the same time Chinese religious beliefs and practices were also influenced by, and intermingled with, the host country religious beliefs and practices e.g. the incorporation of a local Malay name for a deity believed to have inhabited a particular tree, rock, etc.

The places of worship of the Chinese and Indian immigrants have architectural styles which are starkly different from each other and also from those of the local inhabitants. For example, there is no difficulty in distinguishing between a Chinese or Indian temple or an imported European architectural style of Christian church from that of a local Malay mosque in either Singapore or Malaysia.

It was that kind of diverse social, political and religious environment which the early Baha'is confronted when they arrived to promulgate the Baha'i Faith.

---

30   Also migrating there were people from India (mainly Tamils from southern India and Sri Lanka).

China, China, China-ward . . .

"China, China, China-ward the Cause of Baha'u'llah must march! Where is that holy, sanctified Baha'i to become the teacher of China! China has most great capability. The Chinese people are most simple-hearted and truth-seeking. The Baha'i teacher of the Chinese people must first be imbued with their spirit, know their sacred literature, study their national customs and speak to them from their own stand-point, and their own terminologies. He must entertain no thought of his own, but ever think of their spiritual welfare. In China one can teach many souls and train and educate such divine personages that each one of them may become the bright candle of the world of humanity. Truly I say the Chinese are free from any deceit and hypocrisies and are prompted with ideal motives. Had I been feeling well I would have taken a journey to China myself . . ." [31].

At the beginning of this century while He was still in imprisonment and exile, 'Abdu'l-Baha yearned to travel to China to spread the Cause of Baha'u'llah. He exclaimed: *"O! that I might be confirmed in this! Then I thought I might go to Kashgar, one of the provinces of China and a place not visited up to that time by any Baha'i teacher. I was going to travel alone and with no baggage — only a handbag containing a number of tablets and books and papers and pens. I secured even my passport: the old Mofti stood as my guarantor".* 'Abdu'l-Baha's desire was deterred by the crafty Mufti[32] of Akka[33], Ibrahim Pasha[34], who sent his secretary with a message to 'Abdu'l-Baha stating: *"I heard that your Excellency contemplates taking a long journey. I will not be so disrespectful or discourteous as to thwart your plan or in any way hinder your departure but, as I am the Governor of this province, I am responsible to the central government for everything that happens here. Therefore, it will be but my official duty to send a cable concerning your departure as soon as you set your feet on the steamer!"* [35]. Abdu'l-Baha understood from the message of the Mufti that He was not to be allowed to leave Akka for China. 'Abdu'l-Baha then goes on to state: *"China is the country of the future. I hope the right kind of teacher will be inspired to go to that vast empire to lay the foundation of the Kingdom of God, to promote the principles of divine civilization, to unfurl the banner of the Cause of Baha'u'llah . . ."* [36].

---

31   'Abdu'l-Baha in *Star of the West, Vol. 13*. George Ronald, Oxford, 1984, pp.185-186.
32   A consulting canon lawyer in Sunni Islam.
33   Arabic name for port city of Akko, the prison-city of the Turkish Empire in the nineteenth
      century. Baha'u'llah, accompanied by His family and companions, arrived in Akka, Palestine
      (now Israel) in 1868. Designated by Baha'u'llah as the 'Most Great Prison'.
34   Turkish high-ranking officer.
35   *Star of the West, Vol. 13*. George Ronald, Oxford, 1984, pp.185-186.
36   *ibid*

'Abdu'l-Baha in Adrianople
(Baha'u'llah: The King of Glory, H.M. Balyuzi, p.234)

'Akka, the Most Great Prison

Jamal Effendi with an unidentified boy of the Indian subcontinent
(Eminent Baha'is In the time of Baha'u'llah, H.M. Balyuzi, p.123)

The Early Teachers

Two early believers of the Baha'i Faith significantly contributed to the teaching of the Faith in the region. The first was Jamal Effendi[37], also known as the Conqueror of India. He contributed significantly to the expansion of the Baha'i Faith in India and Burma. Jamal Effendi travelled and taught extensively in the Indian subcontinent and other regions bordering China. After visiting Baha'u'llah in the Holy Land, Jamal Effendi was directed by Him to return to the Indian subcontinent to carry on his teaching work and to travel further afield. In 1888, accompanied by Haji Faraju'llah-i-Tafrishi, an exile from Akka, he embarked on a long journey to the East, visiting many countries including Burma, Java[38], Siam (now Thailand) and Singapore[39]. They also travelled in the remote northern regions of Asia, visiting Kashmir, Tibet (now Xizang Autonomous Region), Yarqand (now Suoche, China) and Khuqand in Chinese Turkistan (now Kokand, U.S.S.R.) and then to Badakhshan and Balkh in Afghanistan. At present no information has come to light about local people becoming Baha'is in those regions but certainly many people became Baha'is in India and Burma.

---

37 Sulayman Khan Ilyas (H.M. Balyuzi. *Eminent Baha'is: In the time of Baha'u'llah.* George Ronald, Oxford, 1985, pp.116-128).

38 Formerly part of the Dutch East Indies (now Indonesia).

39 Founded by Thomas Stamford Raffles in 1819.

The other devoted follower of Baha'u'llah to play an important role at that time in the promotion of the Baha'i Faith in the Indo-Asiatic region was Siyyid[40] Mustafa Rumi[41], an eminent associate of Jamal Effendi who was converted to the Baha'i Faith by him in Madras in 1875. Siyyid Mustafa Rumi arrived in Burma in 1878 and settled in Rangoon. He remained in Burma to build up the Burmese Baha'i community and to further teach the Cause. Mustafa Rumi passed away in Burma in 1945 and was posthumously appointed a Hand of the Cause of God[42] by the Guardian, Shoghi Effendi. One of the most significant contributions of Siyyid Mustafa Rumi in Burma was the enrolment of the entire village of Daidanaw in the Baha'i Faith. It was the Burmese Baha'is who contributed the marble sarcophagus that contains the holy remains of the Bab[43], the Forerunner of Baha'u'llah.

Siyyid Mustafa Rumi, builder of the Burmese community
(Eminent Baha'is In the time of Baha'u'llah, H.M. Balyuzi, p.127)

Later it will be shown how the spiritual descendants of those two great teachers of the Cause further contributed to the promulgation of the Baha'i Faith in the countries of the Far East and Southeast Asia.

---

40   Descendant of prophet Muhammad.
41   In 1899 he carried to the Holy Land, with other Baha'is, the marble sarcophagus made by the Baha'is of Mandalay for the Holy Remains of the Bab. He passed away at the age of 99 in 1945 (see *The Baha'i World Vol X*, pp.517-520).
42   Hands of the Cause of God are individuals appointed by Baha'u'llah and later Shoghi Effendi for the purpose of protecting and propagating the Baha'i Faith.
43   Forerunner of Baha'u'llah and Prophet-Founder of the Babi Faith. Born Siyyid 'Ali-Muhammad in Shiraz, Iran, on 20 October 1819. Declared Himself on 23 May 1844 as one of the Twin messengers of God as prophesied in all the holy scriptures. Martyred in Tabriz, Iran, on 9 July 1850. Holy remains now rest on Mount Carmel, Haifa, Israel.

First Baha'i in China

The first record of a Baha'i living in China is of a cousin of the Bab, Haji[44] Mirza[45] Muhammad-'Ali[46], the eldest son of Haji Mirza Siyyid Muhammad[47]. Haji Mirza Muhammad-'Ali[48] lived in Shanghai from 1862 to 1868. From 1870 he resided as a merchant in Hong Kong dealing mainly in Chinese porcelain. Among his clients were the notables of Iran including Nasiri'Din Shah. His commercial enterprise in China and Hong Kong involved the export of tea, porcelain wares, and gold items. Three silver and gold picture frames made in China were offered by Haji Mirza Muhammad-'Ali for the photographs of Baha'u'llah. A number of tablets addressed by Baha'u'llah to Haji Mirza Muhammad-'Ali and his brother Haji Mirza Muhammad Husayn[49] indicate that such items as tea chests, chinaware, tea, preserves, cinnamon, flower seeds, spectacles, specially made writing paper and cloths were sent by the two Afnans[50] from China and were received in the Holy Land[51]. Haji Mirza Muhammad-'Ali passed away in Bombay in 1897 on his way back to Shiraz. In that period the Afnans had commercial enterprises in various cities ranging from Hong Kong to Baku on the Caspian sea. A nephew of the wife of the Bab, Aqa Mirza Ibrahim, also resided in Hong Kong in the period 1881-1882.

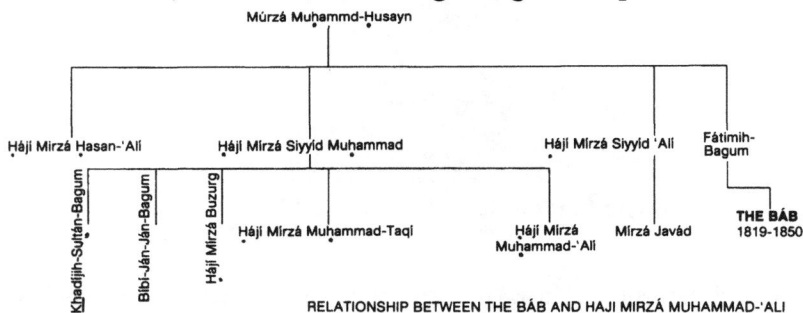

Múrzá Muḥammd-Ḥusayn
— Hájí Mirzá Ḥasan-'Alí
    — Khadijih-Sultán-Bagum
    — Bibi-Ján-Ján-Bagum
    — Hájí Mirzá Buzurg
— Hájí Mirzá Siyyid Muhammad
    — Hájí Mirzá Muhammad-Taqí
— Hájí Mirzá Siyyid 'Alí
    — Hájí Mirzá Muhammad-'Alí
    — Mirzá Javád
    — THE BÁB 1819-1850
— Fátimih-Bagum

RELATIONSHIP BETWEEN THE BÁB AND HAJI MIRZÁ MUḤAMMAD-'ALI

44   Muslim who had made the pilgrimage to Mecca.
45   Means 'mister' when placed before a name and 'prince' if placed after a name.
46   H.M. Balyuzi. *Baha'u'llah, the King of Glory*. George Ronald, Oxford, 1980, p.388.
47   Eldest uncle of the Bab (also known as Khal-i-Akbar). The *Kitab-i-Iqan* was revealed to him by Baha'u'llah in response to his questions.
48   Notes prepared by Research Department, Baha'i World Centre, 9 March 1990.
49   Known as Haji Mirza Buzurg. The third and youngest child of Haji Mirza Siyyid Muhammad. He settled in Hong Kong with his business partner and brother, Haji Mirza Muhammad-'Ali, together establishing a trading company in China.
50   Descendants of the three maternal uncles of the Bab, and of the two brothers of His wives.
51   Some of these items are on display in the Baha'i International Archives in Haifa, Israel. Also to be seen at the Baha'i World Centre are various pieces of Chinese furniture and artifacts which were bought by Shoghi Effendi.

Arrival of More Baha'is in China

It was not until 1902 that two Persian Baha'is, Aqa Mirza Mihdi Rashti and Aqa Mirza 'Abdu'l-Baqi Yazdi, arrived in Shanghai, China, from 'Ishqabad[52], to open a branch of the Ummi'd company, an import-export firm[53]. In one of the letters of Shoghi Effendi dated 7 June 1919, he wrote that Aqa Mirza Mihdi Rashti was amongst the first group of pilgrims who had just arrived from Turkestan and the Caucasus; and that Mirza Rashti had reported: *"Shanghai is awakened. Chinese people are converted and bestow in their turn the Light to their fellow men".* Martha Root[54], in a letter to Shoghi Effendi dated 1 January 1924, mentioned that Aqa Mirza Mihdi Rashti had passed away in Shanghai[55].

In 1910 two Baha'is from the United States, Charles M. Remey[56] and Howard C. Struven, visited Shanghai and met Aqa Mirza 'Abdu'l-Baqi Yazdi. They were probably the first Baha'is from the West to visit China. In that period the Baha'i community in China was still essentially just the two Persian believers who had opened the branch of the Ummi'd company.

---

52   Ashkabad in Russian Turkistan. Once a location of a large Baha'i community and the site of the first Baha'i House of Worship.

53   Notes prepared by Research Department, Baha'i World Centre, 9 March 1990.

54   10 August 1872 — 28 September 1939. Shoghi Effendi stated: *"Posterity will establish her as foremost Hand which 'Abdu'l-Baha's will has raised up first Baha'i century".* (M.R. Garis. *Martha Root, Lioness at the Threshold.* Baha'i Publishing Trust, Wilmette, Illinois, 1983, p.490). Appointed posthumously a Hand of the Cause of God by Shoghi Effendi.

55   *ibid*

56   Hand of the Cause of God who became a Covenant-breaker (one who undermines the Covenant of the Baha'i Faith) after the passing of the Guardian.

A group of Bahá'ís in Shanghai, China *circa* March or April 1930 Seated (left to right): One of Mr. Ouskoui's younger daughters, either Ruhania (Rawhaniyyih) or Jalalia (Jalaliyyih), Sarah, Mr. Ouskoui's mother, Mrs. Ridvaniyyih Suleimani (Mr. Ouskoui's daughter and Mr. Suleimani's wife) Standing (left to right): Mr. Husayn Ouskoui (Husayn Usku'i), One of Mr. Ouskoui's younger daughters, either Ruhania (Rawhaniyyih) or Jalalia (Jalaliyyih), Mirza Hossein Touty (Mirza Husayn Tuti), Mr. Suleiman Suleimani, Goudrat (Qudrat, Mr. Ouskoui's son) (The Bahá'í World Vol. III p.361)

Dr. Sun Yat-sen, Father of the Republic of China. Martha Root proclaimed the Baha'i Faith to him in 1924
(Courtesy Sun Yat-Sen: Frustrated Patriot, C. Martin Wilbur)

In 1914[57] with the arrival in Shanghai of Husayn Uskuli[58] and two other Baha'is, the Baha'i Faith began to be more firmly established in China. Husayn Uskuli[59] later brought his family to join him in Shanghai. He was born in 1875 in the township of Usku in Adhirbayjan, and had learned the Baha'i Faith from the renowned Baha'i teacher, Haji Mirza Haydar-'Ali[60]. Husayn Uskuli also had the bounty of attaining pilgrimage during the lifetime of 'Abdu'l-Baha. After his marriage, Husayn Uskuli moved with his wife to 'Ishqabad, remaining there for many years before pioneering to China. The home of the Uskulis in Shanghai was the main meeting place of the Baha'is and a place of warm hospitality to visitors. In 1931 Mr. and Mrs. Uskuli lived at 451 Kiangse Road, Shanghai, with their daughter and son-in-law, Mr. and Mrs. Suleimani. By then, a Baha'i community had been established in Shanghai[61], as evident from photographs taken in that city. A number of Chinese became Baha'is, and presumably the first Local Spiritual Assembly[62] of Shanghai was formed in 1928, with the Kiangse Road address of the Uskulis listed as the correspondence address of the Baha'i Faith in China[63]. The address of Tswi (Tsui) Pei, Manager of the Bank of China, was listed as the correspondence address of the Baha'i Group in Hong Kong in the same year64. Not much is known about Tswi Pei.

Husayn Uskuli's services to the Cause in China were numerous, including acting as the main link between the Baha'is in China and the Guardian, Shoghi Effendi. For example, in 1925 the Guardian cabled Mr. Uskuli requesting him to cable the British High Commissioner in Baghdad to implore on behalf of the Baha'is in China his assistance in enforcing justice concerning the ownership of Baha'u'llah's house, which was occupied by the enemies of the Faith. Husayn Uskuli visited Taiwan[65] in 1935 to purchase tea for his import-export business. He is the first Baha'i reported to have visited there. Despite extreme danger to his life during the war years of 1937-1945 and the difficult conditions following

---

57   Agnes Alexander sailed from France in September to go to Japan for the first time, stopping
      over in Hong Kong in October.
58   Since he came from the township of Usku, in all probability his name was Usku'i in the Persian
      format.
59   *The Baha'i World Vol. XIII,* pp.871-873.
60   Known as 'Angel of Mount Carmel'. Passed away in Haifa in 1920.
61   *The Baha'i World Vol. III,* p.361.
62   Locally elected Baha'i administrative body.
63   *The Baha'i World Vol. II,* p.182, 185.
64   Notes prepared by Research Department, Baha'i World Centre, 9 March 1990.
65   Formosa.

the victory of the Chinese Communist Party, Mr. Uskuli remained faithfully in his pioneering post as the only known foreign Baha'i in Shanghai, enduring many difficulties and much hardship. The Guardian had written to him expressing the great importance of his remaining in Shanghai but he also cautioned him to be discreet in his teaching activities lest his position as a Baha'i be jeopardised. Many Western Baha'is had already left China and many of his Chinese contacts did not visit him for fear of being suspected by the Chinese authorities of being in collaboration with foreigners. China was going through a difficult transitional period of adjustment to the new Communist government. Inflation was rampant and civil war was still looming. Foreigners, especially Westerners, were viewed with suspicion. This xenophobic attitude of the Chinese government remained for many years. Mr. Uskuli passed away in Shanghai on 25 February 1956 at the age of eight-two, leaving behind four daughters and a son. He is buried in the Kiangwan Cemetery in Shanghai.

Chinese Baha'is in China

The earliest record shows that the first Chinese Baha'i in China was Mr. Chen Hai An[66] (who called himself Harold A. Chen in the United States). He studied at the University of Chicago and left in mid-June 1916 to study Public

Dr. Zia Bagdadi, instrumental in guiding the first Chinese Baha'i, Chen Hai An, into the Faith
(The Baha'i World Vol. VII p.536)

---

66   Notes prepared by Research Department, Baha'i World Centre, 9 March 1990.

Law at Columbia University in New York. Chen returned to his birthplace in Shanghai, sailing from San Francisco on 22 December 1916. He had become a Baha'i in Chicago some time in April or early May 1919 through the love and guidance of Mr. Zia Bagdadi[67]. Mr. Roy Wilhelm[68], in a letter dated 20 October 1916 to Mrs. Ella Cooper[69], described Chen as *"a six months old Baha'i baby of Zia Bagdadi"*. From the moment he became a Baha'i, Chen showed great enthusiasm in the promotion of his newly found Cause. In a letter dated 4 May 1916 to an Ernest Walters written on official stationary of the Pan-Asiatic League of the University of Chicago, he wrote: *"I am trying to spread my newly-gained gospel among three thousand students in this University (University of Chicago)"*. Chen's enthusiasm can again be noted in another letter to Ernest Walters dated 19 December 1916, which he wrote prior to his departure from San Francisco for China: *"I shall sail on Dec. 22nd. Do please pray for me that God will guide me in my work. I shall see Mr. Bahi, a Persian Baha'i in Shanghai, and we shall try to establish a Chinese Baha'i assembly there"*. In that same year Mr. Anthony Yuen Seto[70] and his wife Mamie Loretta O'Connor[71] became Baha'is in Hawaii. Mr. Seto became the first Chinese Baha'i in the Hawaiian Islands and the first Chinese-American Baha'i in the United States.

On 31 July 1915, the world famous Baha'i travelling teacher Martha Root sailed from Yokohama for the Hawaiian Islands, stopping briefly in Manchuria[72]. That appears to have been the first time she reached the shores of China. Her passport indicated that China was one of the countries she intended to visit. It is not known whether she carried out any teaching activities during her brief stop-over. Nevertheless, Martha Root subsequently made three other visits to China, which were to have significant impact on the history of the Baha'i Faith there.

---

67   Arrived in United States from Persia in September 1909 to study medicine. A great Baha'i teacher. Passed away in 1937 (see *The Baha'i World Vol. VII*, pp.535-539).

68   17 September 1875 – 20 December 1951. Served many years on the Baha'i Temple Unity Committee and the National Spiritual Assembly of the Baha'is of United States and Canada. A close friend of Martha Root (see *The Baha'i World Vol. XII*, pp.662-664).

69   Renowned American believer who, on 10 December 1898, was among the first Western pilgrims to visit the Holy Land.

70   18 November 1890 – 6 May 1957. A lawyer. Elected Chairman of the first Spiritual Assembly of Honolulu (see *The Baha'i World Vol. XIII*, p.886-889).

71   10 April 1885 – 15 April 1970 (see *The Baha'i World Vol. XV*, pp.479-481).

72   M.R. Garis. *Martha Root, Lioness at the Threshold*. Baha'i Publishing Trust, Wilmette, Illinois, 1983, pp.58, 70 and 71.

In 1917 eleven Persian Baha'is assembled in Shanghai. Mainly through the effort of two of them, Aqa Mirza Ahmad and Radi Tabrizi, a Baha'i pamphlet was published, probably the first Baha'i publication in the Chinese language. It included *Twelve Baha'i Principles,* and passages from 'Abdu'l-Baha's explanation of the spiritual significance of the European War, which had previously been translated by a Korean Baha'i into Chinese. The pamphlet, which included a picture of 'Abdu'l-Baha, was also published in Persian. A year later, a brief explanation of the Baha'i Faith in Russian was made available by Aqa Mirza Ahmad Radi Tabrizi in Kharbin (now Harbin), Manchuria (now Heilungkiang Province, China).

In 1919 another mainland Chinese, Chen Ting Mo, accepted the Baha'i Faith in the United States. Chen was equally enthusiastic about his newly found Faith and brought back to China many Baha'i books, which he deposited in a library in Shanghai. Chen had the bounty of receiving a Tablet from 'Abdu'l-Baha in which he was exhorted to *"consolidate the assembly thou hast established at Shanghai as well as the one instituted at Peking*[73]. *Engage in the promulgation of the Cause of God."* 'Abdu'l-Baha further asked Chen to convey on His behalf *"the utmost love and kindness"* to *"the two newly-converted souls"* for whom He would *"beg confirmation that they may personify the bounty of God, may be guided, may become two ignited candles and may bestow upon China a heavenly light."* There seems to be no other reference to the establishment in that period of a Baha'i community in Beijing. Presumably one of *"the two newly-converted souls"* was Mr. Chen Hai An but information is not available about the identity of the other.

Martha Root and the Early Baha'is

On 25 April 1923 Martha Root left Osaka, Japan, for northern China. That was her second visit to China and it lasted almost a year to March 1924. In Beijing she stayed at a guest house called Ping an Fang, 'House of Peace', which was managed by a British woman doctor. Martha Root engaged in various forms of Baha'i activities, including giving numerous talks and lectures at nearly one hundred universities, colleges and schools[74], holding public meetings, and proclaiming the Baha'i Faith to many individuals and people of importance. Some of those prominent people included the adviser to President of the

---

73   Beijing.
74   Shoghi Effendi. *God Passes By.* Baha'i Publishing Trust, Wilmette, Illinois, 1970, p.387.

Chinese Republic, Li Yuan-hung[75]. She also wrote many articles on the Baha'i Faith for such newspapers as the 'English Standard' and the 'North China Standard'. Some of those articles were published in both English and Chinese. She also tutored and taught English to many Chinese students, taught twice at Yenching[76] Women's College and worked as a teaching assistant in an Esperanto[77] school in Beijing. Several exchanges of letters occurred between the Guardian, Shoghi Effendi, and some of those students of Martha Root. Martha also tried to learn Chinese in order to be more effective in teaching the people while she was in Beijing but she did not have enough spare time to master it. Mrs. Ida Finch, who was visiting Miss Agnes Alexander[78] in Japan, joined Martha Root in Beijing. Mrs. Finch remained in China until 19 August 1923 and then left for Tokyo. Shortly afterwards, Mrs. Finch left that city by ship for Seattle in the United States.

---

75 Succeeded Yuan Shih-k'ai, the first president of the Kuomintang Nationalist Party. Li's four years as president had far-reaching effect for China as his administration destroyed the chances for construction of a new republic, was corrupt and responsible for the spread of warlordism to every part of the country. The warlord rule from 1916-18 made it more difficult for China to resist further foreign aggression and the recovery of her full sovereignty.

76 Former name of Peking and one of the capitals of the Chin dynasty (1125-1234 A.D).

77 Many early Baha'is learnt Esperanto because of the Baha'i Faith's advocacy of an international auxiliary language. Esperanto was created by Dr. Ludwik Zamenhof, whose daughter Lidia became a Baha'i through a meeting with Martha Root (see Wendy Heller. *Lidia: The Life of Lidia Zamenhof Daughter of Esperanto.* George Ronald, Oxford, 1985). The first all-Esperanto university in the world was opened in Beijing in September 1923, enroling 170 students from all over the world.

78 Agnes Baldwin Alexander. Born in Hawaii on 21 July 1875. Accepted the Baha'i Faith in Paris on 26 November 1900, and on returning to Hawaii, became the first Baha'i on the island. Received a Tablet from 'Abdu'l-Baha on 13 October 1913 encouraging her to travel to Japan. Arrived in Japan in 1914 and remained there for a total of thirty-two years. Was also the first Baha'i to teach in Korea, and is mentioned in the Tablet of the Divine Plan. Visited China, Korea, Taiwan, Hong Kong, Philippines, United States, Canada and Europe. Left Japan in 1937, returning in 1950. Appointed a Hand of the Cause of God by Shoghi Effendi on 27 March 1957. Member of the first National Spiritual Assembly of the Baha'is of Northeast Asia with its seat in Tokyo. Returned to Hawaii from Japan in 1967 and passed away in Hawaii on 1 January 1971 (see *The Baha'i World Vol. XV,* pp.423-430).

Martha Root (seated, front row), with Mr. Fukuta, the first Baha'i in Japan (front row, far left). Agnes Alexander is standing in the back row *circa* 1915.
(Martha Root: Lioness at the Threshold, M.R. Garis, p.69)

Martha Root travelled extensively in China accompanied by Agnes Alexander and her sister Mary, who was not a Baha'i. Martha's companions had come from Japan to join her for two months on 12 October 1923 following a earthquake there on 1 September. They held a Baha'i Feast together in Beijing on 4 November 1923, the first recorded in that city. One of the many influential Chinese Martha Root and Agnes Alexander was able to meet in Beijing was Mr. Pao[79], then working as a secretary to General Feng[80]. As a result of the acquaintance they were able to proclaim the Baha'i Faith at a school run by General Feng for the military officers' children. Another influential Chinese they met was Mr. P.W. Chen, who first heard of the Baha'i Faith through reading Baha'i books brought back to Shanghai from Japan by Mr. Pao in 1920. On request from Mr. Pao, Mr. Chen helped translate some of the Baha'i books for a newspaper article. It was through the assistance of Mr. Chen that Martha Root and Agnes Alexander were able to speak at a large gathering in Beijing and to meet Mr. Deng Chieh-ming. Deng became attracted to the Baha'i Faith and later became a Baha'i. He also expressed his desire to open a Baha'i College in Beijing, which he was able to do prior to the departure of Martha Root from China. Besides the usual curriculum, daily lectures in Esperanto were given.

79   He had earlier met Agnes Alexander in Japan.
80   Most probably the famous Christian General Feng Yu-hsiang (1882-1948). Supporter of Sun Yat-sen's nationalist programme.

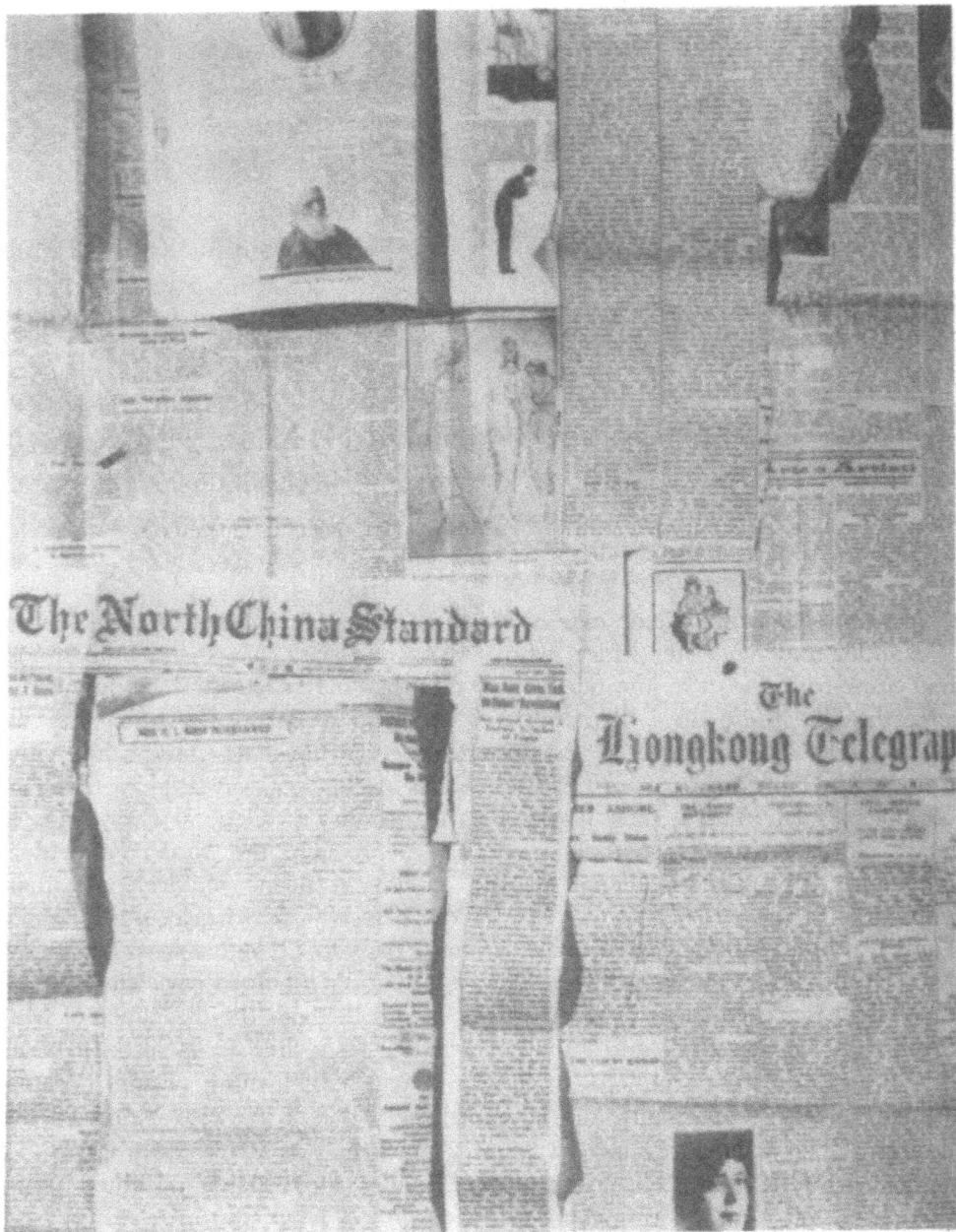

Newspaper articles written by Martha Root proclaiming the Baha'i Faith in China and Hong Kong
(Martha Root: Lioness at the Threshold, M.R. Garis, p.360)

Martha Root, Agnes Alexander and her sister Mary, accompanied by Deng, left Beijing on 25 November 1923 to travel to the northeastern region of China, visiting many cities including Tientsin, Ginanfu (now Chin-Ch'eng) where they spoke at the Shantung Christian College, Chefoo (now Yentai) the birthplace of Confucius, and Tsuchowfu. They later travelled by rail to Shanghai via Nanking (Nanjing), which is situated on the Yangtze River, and Soochow (Suzhou). On reaching Shanghai, Agnes and Mary sailed for Honolulu, Hawaii, on 27 December 1923 but Martha stayed on in Shanghai for two and a half months. She spoke to a number of groups there, including the Confucian Association, the Theosophists and the Esperantists. She again had opportunities to write articles on the Baha'i Faith for newspapers such as the 'Shanghai Times', and travelled inland to Wuchang and Hangchow (now Hangzhou) to teach the Baha'i Faith. Martha left Shanghai for Hong Kong on 27 March 1924.

After arriving in Hong Kong at the beginning of April 1924, Martha Root was again busy in her teaching activities, visiting editors of local newspapers, presidents of universities, and librarians; giving numerous talks and lectures; and meeting a number of prominent people. The 'Hong Kong Telegraph' published an editorial on Martha Root and the Baha'i Faith because she had made a good impression while in Hong Kong. She spoke at the Hong Kong University where she was also able to proclaim the Faith to one of India's most famous poets, the educator and humanist Rabindranath Tagore[81], who was visiting China. From Hong Kong Martha Root ventured again into mainland China, visiting Canton (now Guangzhou) where she had the opportunity to give a number of talks. She returned to Hong Kong and took a four-day trip by ship down the coast to spent a week in Saigon, the capital city of Vietnam. Martha also briefly visited Cambodia (French Indo-China[82]). In Indo-China she was again successful in having her articles on the Baha'i Faith published in both the local Chinese and Vietnamese newspapers, and was able to speak at a school where the students had come from diverse religious backgrounds. She returned to Hong Kong at the end of May 1924 and then sailed for Australia and New Zealand. Martha Root's efforts in writing articles on the Baha'i Faith for the newspapers resulted in the wide proclamation of the Faith not only in China and Hong Kong but also in the Philippines because the Chinese newspapers were also sent there.

---

81 Tagore received a Nobel Prize in 1913. Visited China in 1924 on invitation by Chinese intellectuals Xu Zhimo, Liang Qichao and Zhang Junmai under the sponsorship of their Society for Lectures on the New Learning.

82 Vietnam, Laos and Cambodia.

Martha arrived in Melbourne, Australia, in late June or early July, travelling by rail to join Clara and Hyde Dunn[83] in Perth. There she met a group of local Chinese when they came to the Library Institute to listen to her lecture on 'The Great Renaissance of China'. She gave the same lecture in Auckland, New Zealand, at the large auditorium of the Society of Arts. While in that country she had the opportunity to address the Chinese Nationalist Clubs in both Auckland and Wellington.

The most significant event of Martha Root's visit during her second visit to China was the acceptance of the Baha'i Faith by Dr. Y.S. Tsao (Tsao Yun-siang), the President of the Xinhua (Tsing Hua) University[84] in Beijing. Agnes Alexander[85] said that Martha Root was brave in going to the Xinhua University without the customary introduction, but she was kindly received by Dr. Tsao and his wife. Dr. Tsao was a 1911 graduate of Yale University in the United States and had also studied at Harvard. His Swedish-born wife, Elin Louise Halling86, who was an American citizen, also became a Baha'i in the same period. They moved to Shanghai after eight years of teaching at Xinhua University and formed close bonds with the Persian Baha'is there. Martha Root[87] met Dr. Tsao again in 1930 in Canton. In their conversation Dr. Tsao expounded upon the relevance of the Baha'i Faith to China in light of the present turmoil, and upon the significance of the advent of Baha'u'llah, by pointing out that Confucius had taught that a great teacher or reformer would appear every five hundred years or so.

Dr. Tsao later translated many Baha'i books and pamphlets into the Chinese language, among them Dr. John E. Esslemont's[88] book *Baha'u'llah and the New Era* in 1931. The preface of that book was written by Rev. K.T. Chung[89], a junior of Dr. Tsao, who not only saluted the principles enunciated in the Baha'i Faith but concluded his preface by stating: *"Should everybody again exert his efforts towards the extension of this beneficent influence throughout the world, it will then bring about world peace and the general welfare of humanity"*[90]. Before he

---

83   Hands of the Cause of God instrumental in the establishment of the Baha'i Faith in Australia and New Zealand (see *The Baha'i World Vol. IX*, pp.593-596).

84   A Boxer Indemnity Institution.

85   *The Baha'i World Vol. VII*, p.548.

86   They met and married in London as Dr. Tsao was serving there for the Chinese government.

87   *The Baha'i World Vol. IV*, p.432.

88   Dr. John E. Esslemont was appointed posthumously as a Hand of the Cause of God by Shoghi Effendi. Passed away in the Holy Land in 1925.

89   Greatly admired the Baha'i Faith and Dr. Y.S. Tsao.

90   *The Baha'i World Vol. IV*, pp.420-428.

could render more services to the Faith, Dr. Tsao passed away in Shanghai after a car accident on his way home on 8 February, 1937. Mrs. Tsao moved to live in Beijing in 1938. Three years before his untimely death, Dr. Tsao completed a major part of the translation into Chinese of *Some Answered Questions* [91]. Mr. Tang T.Y., a friend of Dr. Tsao, who was making corrections of the translation of *Some Answered Questions,* passed away shortly after the death of Dr. Tsao. As a result, in 1937, Mr. Shen I.S. had to translate chapters 39 to 44 of Dr. Tsao's manuscript as they had been lost. On 12 November 1939 the translation of *Some Answered Questions* was finally printed in Shanghai [92].

Martha Root in Shanghai, 1 July 1937, prior to the bombings which forced her to leave in late August
(Martha Root: Lioness at the Threshold, M.R. Garis, p.442)

---

91   Compilation of questions posed to 'Abdu'l-Baha by Laura Clifford Barney during several visits to Akka in 1904-6.

92   A list of Baha'i publications in Chinese can be obtained from *The Baha'i World' Vols. VI,* p.549, VIII, p.738 and *X,* p.615.

John E. Esslemont, author of Baha'u'llah and the New Era, which Dr. Ẏ.S. Tsao translated into Chinese
(The Baha'i World Vol. XIV p.447)

In 1923, the daughter and son-in-law of Mr. Uskuli[93], Ridvaniyyih[94] and 'Ali-Muhammad Suleimani[95], arrived in Shanghai as pioneers[96]. Together with the Uskulis they were to render many invaluable services to the Faith. They left Shanghai in August 1950 due to the difficult conditions prevailing then in China, and returned to Iran. They later pioneered to Taiwan, arriving in Keelung on 22 October 1954, becoming the first overseas Baha'is to settle there. At the time of their arrival there were already ten local believers. Two years later the first Local Spiritual Assembly of Taiwan was formed in Tainan.

In 1926 another Chinese, Mr. Zhi, accepted the Baha'i Faith through the teaching work of Mrs. Ida Finch, who was visiting Martha Root from Japan to help with the teaching work. Mr. Zhi printed a booklet called *Magazine*[97] in China but not much is known of his Baha'i activities. In 1933, Husayn Uskuli reported that Mr. Zhi's brother had also become a Baha'i.

In 1930 Martha Root made her third visit to China, staying two months. That time she arrived via Hong Kong and stayed for a week in Canton where she broadcast lectures over the Canton radio and lectured at Sun Yat-sen University and secondary schools. She published three translated radio broadcast lectures, 'New Universal Language', 'Esperanto As a Universal Language' and 'What is the Baha'i Movement?' in a special two-page-spread supplement of the 'Canton Municipal Daily News' on 23 September 1930. The supplement also featured a photograph of 'Abdu'l-Baha. In Hong Kong Martha Root concentrated mainly on writing articles on the Baha'i Faith rather than giving lectures, and was able to publish thirty articles during her short stay. She also met Mr. Chen Ming-shu, the then Governor of Kwangtung (now Guangdong) Province. Chan S. Liu and his sister Mrs. Foulk I.W. served as Martha's interpreter (*refer to later sections for details*). In her article 'Chinese

---

93 The Husayn Uskuli family in this period included his mother, Sarah Khanum; his eldest
    daughter, Mrs. Ridvaniyyih Suleimani; and son-in-law, Mr. Suleiman Suleimani (Sulayman
    'Ali-Muhammad Sulayman Milani); and his two younger daughters, Ruhania (Rawhaniyyih)
    and Jalalia (Jalaliyyih), and his son Goudrat (Qudrat). In 1934 Ruhania, Jalalia and Goudrat left
    Shanghai with their paternal grandmother, Sarah Khanum, to study at the American University
    in Beirut.

94 Served on different occasions as an Auxiliary Board Member and member of the National
    Spiritual Assembly of Taiwan. Passed away in Taiwan on 18 March 1981 (see *The Baha'i
    World Vol. XVIII*, pp.738-740)

95 Sulayman 'Ali-Muhammad Sulaymani Milani. Passed away in Taiwan in 1988.

96 *The Baha'i World Vol. XVIII*, p.752.

97 It was common for intellectuals to publish magazines, periodicals, etc. in China during that
    period.

Culture and Baha'ism'[98], Martha Root described General Chen as a man with vision and one who thought deeply. Chen was reported to say: *"I did not know much about this Baha'i Movement until you sent me a booklet two days ago, but as I read it, I believe Baha'u'llah was a Prophet and China has need of a Prophet in these days. Such Teachings at their lowest estimate could not harm any nation and at their highest they could do great good in China and in every other country. No nation is more fitted to receive these Teachings than China, for the base of Chinese civilization is universal peace. Just now we are going through great disturbances, but when China is righted and we are on an equal footing with other nations, China will take her place in all international welfare."* From Canton Martha Root travelled to Shanghai where she was again joined by Agnes Alexander, who had come from Japan in the latter part of September to assist with the teaching work. Mr. Uskuli and his two daughters, as well as Mr. Suleimani, Mr. Mirza Husayn Tuti[99], and Dr. and Mrs. Tsao were in Shanghai when Agnes Alexander arrived. Martha and Agnes gave three lectures at the Royal Asiatic Society. Martha also submitted a number of articles for publication to all the local newspapers, and they published stories on the Baha'i Faith for eight consecutive days. Martha and Agnes spent ten days together teaching the Faith in Shanghai. Martha travelled to Nanking for a week, accompanied by Mr. Suleimani. In Nanking she gave a lecture, 'International Education For the New Age', to a predominantly male audience at the National Central University on 6 October 1930. The few female students present were excited to learn of the Baha'i teaching of the equality of men and women[100]. She also spoke at the Ginling College for Women and met a number of government officials. Martha then returned to Shanghai to bid farewell to Agnes Alexander, who sailed for Tokyo on 7 October 1930. During Martha's trip to Shanghai and Nanking she had little access to radio because the broadcasting studios were closed due to the increasing conflict between the Chinese Communist Party and the Nationalist Government. It is known that ten Baha'is were residing in Shanghai at that time. They were Dr. and Mrs. Y.S. Tsao, Mirza Husayn Tuti, and Mr. Husayn Uskuli and his family. Fortnightly Baha'i meetings were held at the home of the Uskuli's. Dr. Tsao volunteered to translate *Baha'u'llah and the New Era* into Chinese. Martha Root made an initial contribution to the project and promised to raise additional money for

---

98   *Star of the West,* Vol. 21. George Ronald, Oxford, 1984, pp.262-267. Baha'ism is an old term for the Baha'i Faith.

99   Hossein Touty.

100   During this period in China the Chinese women were becoming very aware of woman's suffrage and the need for equality of men and women.

the translation work. She sailed from Shanghai on 22 October 1930 and reached Japan on 27 October. She spent two months there before returning to Hawaii. During that period it was reported that many Chinese scholars had become Baha'is and some of the Cantonese Baha'is translated some of Martha's lectures into Chinese so they could be handed out to the media.

By 1934 the Spiritual Assembly of Shanghai was already firmly established. In a circular letter in May that year, Mr. T.Y. Tang reported that the Assembly comprised eight people, with Mrs. Tsao elected Treasurer and himself Secretary and Librarian.

Agnes Alexander visited the Baha'is in China again on 22 March 1937 when the ship in which she was sailing from Japan to the Holy Land[101] stopped over in Shanghai. She spent one and half days with the Suleimanis, Mr. Uskuli and Mr. Tuti.

In June 1937 Martha Root made her final visit to China, arriving in Shanghai from Japan[102]. In Shanghai Martha lived at the International Settlement[103], a residential area for foreigners. But that time her visit to China was brief because China was at war with Japan. Despite the extreme danger to her life, she was able to renew old friendships and arranged for the shipment of Baha'i literature in both English and Chinese to libraries throughout China as well as to prominent people whom she had met on her previous visits. On 14 August 1937 Martha had to be evacuated because Shanghai was under bombardment from the Japanese occupational forces. The International Settlement was bombed and many lives were lost amidst the ensuing chaos. But when a package containing a Hair of Baha'u'llah fell from Martha's bag, she believed she would reach safety as she recalled from the writings of Baha'u'llah in the *Kitab-i-Iqan that "one Hair of Whose Head is worth more than all in the heavens and the earth".* Mr. Uskuli took her to the wharf to board a tender to go to the President Jefferson liner, which sailed to the Philippines, arriving in Manila on 20 August 1937.

During the period from 1920 to 1940, many Baha'i teachers also visited China, including Mirza Husayn Tuti, Mr. Hippolyte Dreyfus-Barney[104], Mrs.

101　Palestine, now Israel.

102　She was also the last Baha'i to visit Japan until after the end of World War Two.

103　The International Settlement and the French Concession in Shanghai were under direct rule of their foreign residents. That was a condition imposed upon the Qing authorities as a result of the First Opium War.

104　First French Baha'i, who was introduced to the Baha'i Faith by May Bolles Maxwell in 1901, and first European Baha'i to visit Iran. Travelled extensively in Canada and the United States and as far away as Japan. Passed away in 1929.

Baha'is of Shanghai, China *circa* December 1931
Seated (left to right): Mrs. Ridvaniyyih Suleimani, Mrs. Tsao (Elin Louise Halling, Dr. Tsao's wife), Sarah (Mr. Ouskoui's mother), one of Mr. Ouskoui's younger daughters, either Ruhania (Rawhaniyyih) or Jalalia (Jalaliyyih), One of Mr. Ouskoui's younger daughters, either Ruhania (Rawhaniyyih) or Jalalia (Jalaliyyih) Standing (left to right): Mr. Suleiman Suleimani, Mirza Hossein Touty (Mirza Husayn Tuti), Dr. Y.S. Tsao, Mr. Husayn Ouskoui, Goudrat (Qudrat, Mr. Ouskoui's son)
(The Baha'i World Vol. IV p.421)

42

Hand of the Cause of God Mr. Siegfried Schopflocher. Visited China in the 1920s
(The Baha'i World Vol. XII p.665)

M. Hippolyte Dreyfus-Barney, who visited China in the period 1920-22
(The Baha'i World Vol. III p.211)

Keith Ransom-Kehler[105], Mr. F. St. George Spendlove[106], Mr. Mark Tobey[107], Mr. Siegfried Shopflocher[108] and Mrs. Ida Finch.

Keith Ransom-Kehler, a Hand of the Cause of God and first American Baha'i martyr. Visited China in 1931
(The Baha'i World Vol. V p.390)

---

105   Passed away in Isfahan of smallpox on 23 October 1933 and was posthumously appointed Hand of the Cause of God by Shoghi Effendi on 30 October 1933 (see *The Baha'i World Vol. V*, pp.389-400).

106   An expert on Chinese art, who taught himself to read the Chinese language. Passed away in 1962 (see *The Baha'i World Vol. XIII*, pp.895).

107   Famous Baha'i artist with many international awards and accolades. Heard of the Baha'i Faith through Juliet Thompson and became a Baha'i in 1918. He passed away on 26 April 1976 (see *The Baha'i World Vol. XVII*, pp.401-404).

Mirza Husayn Tuti, a Persian Baha'i, arrived in Shanghai in January 1919 and later relocated to the Philippines in 1921. He returned to Shanghai in 1927 and remained there till 1946. He visited Agnes Alexander in Tokyo in 1932[109].

Hippolyte Dreyfus-Barney spent one and a half years in China from 1920 to early 1922.

Keith Ransom-Kehler, who visited Agnes Alexander in Tokyo from 25 June to early August 1931, also visited Shanghai briefly on 12 August 1931 on her way to Australia. While she was in Shanghai, she proclaimed the Faith over the radio, delivered public lectures and conducted a number of interviews with prominent educators and officials. On an invitation from Miss Liu Fung-ling[110] (Chan S. Liu's sister), she visited Canton and was a house guest of Chan S. Liu. She travelled for two years in China, Japan and India before going to Persia in August 1932 on a special mission to represent the American Baha'is in appealing to the Shah's government for removal of the ban on the entry of Baha'i literature into Persia.

108 Visited the Baha'is in the East in conjunction with his business trips. Chiefly responsible for the building of the Wilmette Temple in North America. Called by the Guardian "the Chief Temple Builder". Appointed a Hand of the Cause of God by Shoghi Effendi on 29 February 1952. Passed away on 27 July 1953 in Montreal after a few days illness (see *The Baha'i World Vol. XII,* pp.664-666).

109 He was probably the first Baha'i to visit Japan.

110 Received her Master's degree at the University of Michigan and became Professor of History at Ling Nan University in Canton.

Famous Baha'i potter, Bernard Leach. Visited China with Mark Tobey in 1934
(The Baha'i World Vol. XVIII p.670)

Famous Baha'i painter, Mark Tobey. Visited China with Bernard Leach in 1934
(The Baha'i World Vol. XVII p.401)

F. St. George Spendlove, a Canadian Baha'i, visited Shanghai in 1932 after his pilgrimage to the Holy Land. He travelled to Nanjing and Beijing before proceeding to Japan. In 1934 Mark Tobey, accompanied by Bernard Leach[111], an Englishman who had heard about the Baha'i Faith through him, spent time in Shanghai visiting their friend Teng Kuei from whom Mark had learned the technique and philosophy of Chinese calligraphy when the young Chinese artist was studying at the University of Washington. The ideas and style taught by Teng Kuei were to influence Mark Tobey's paintings in later years. While Mark was in Shanghai he spoke on the history of the Baha'i Faith at the Bankers Club on 11 May 1934. With Dr. Tsao he rented two rooms at the Chinese Y.M.C.A. for the Baha'is of Shanghai to use as a Baha'i Library. The library was closed in 1937. Mark Tobey and Bernard Leach later visited Japan together.

By the 1940s many Chinese in China had heard of the Baha'i Faith and a number of them had become Baha'is. During the Hong Kong Baha'i International Conference in September 1976 the author conversed with an elderly Chinese gentleman who had first heard about the Baha'i Faith in Shanghai in the 1930s.

The Closing Years

From 1920 to 1940 China sent many scholars overseas. They were financed by the Boxer Indemnity Fund to acquire new knowledge and skills for the development of China[112]. Many of those scholars were invited to various Baha'i activities and subsequently some of them became Baha'is. 'Abdu'l-Baha recounted that a Chinese student connected with the Peace Conference in Washington, D.C. attended a Baha'i meeting and asked questions with intense interest. At the close of the session the student said: *"This is the best religion of which I have heard"*. Another Chinese student, whose family were leaders in the new China (i.e. Republic of China), read the Baha'i literature with great enthusiasm and stated: *"This is just what the new China needs"*[113].

---

111 Bernard Leach was not a Baha'i in that period.
112 The majority were sent to Japan.
113 *Star of the West, Vol. 13*. George Ronald, Oxford, 1984, pp.185-186.

'Abdu'l-Baha and Shoghi Effendi in Haifa
(The Mystery of God, p.268)

One of those overseas scholars from China who became a Baha'i was Mr. Chan S. Liu[114] (Liu Chan Song), who studied the Faith with Roy Wilhelm in America. He first heard of the Faith in 1921 while an undergraduate at Cornell University. Keith Ransom-Kehler reported that Liu also attended lectures given by Jenabe Fazel[115]. He accepted the Baha'i Faith that year. He returned to his native city of Canton in the spring of 1923[116] and helped Martha meet many high officials in China. In 1924 he arranged for her to meet Dr. Sun Yat-sen[117],

---

114   Director of Bureau for the Improvement of Sericulture, Department of Reconstruction, in Canton.

115   Mirza Asadu'llah Fadil (1880?-1957), prominent Baha'i teacher and scholar. Was sent by 'Abdu'l-Baha to deepen the knowledge of the Baha'is in Europe and America. Later by Shoghi Effendi to teach in America. (see The Baha'i World Vol. XIV, pp.334-336).

116   During that period in Japan a Chinese student, Mr. H.C. Waung, at the request of Miss Agnes Alexander translated the teaching booklet "9" into Chinese. It was subsequently published and distributed in China.

117   The Baha'i World Vol. IV, p.431.

regarded as the Father of the new Republic of China, acting as her interpreter during the interview. Dr. Sun Yat-sen listened with interest and asked Martha to send him two Baha'i books. Dr. Y.S. Tsao stated in his article 'The Baha'i Cause in China' that Dr. Sun Yat-Sen heard and read about the Baha'i Faith and also declared that it was highly relevant to the needs of China. During that visit of Martha Root, one of Mr. Liu's sisters, Mrs. Foulk I.W., became a Baha'i and also acted as an interpreter for her. In the same year another Chinese, Mr. T.J. Chwang, returned to Shanghai after becoming a Baha'i in Europe.

Chan S. Liu (Liu Chan Song), prominent Chinese Baha'i in China. Director of Bureau for the Improvement of Sericulture, Department of Reconstruction, Honglok, Canton, China
(The Baha'i World Vol. V p.646)

Mr. Liu translated Baha'i literature into the Chinese language. In 1937 he reported to Shoghi Effendi his completion of the translation of *Tablets of Baha'u'llah "after five years of careful work."* Another translation undertaken by Liu was the complete translation of the *Hidden Words* into Chinese. He also printed two thousand copies of a pamphlet of his translation of the 'The Twelve Basic Principles' and a brief history of the Baha'i Faith written by the Guardian. Those translations were then sent by him to numerous libraries in various parts of China. Despite the war when Canton was under bombardment from the Japanese, he was able to write again to the Guardian on 17 June 1938 stating: *"In the midst of bombs and bullets I have completed the translation of two important Baha'i books, namely the* Tablets of Baha'u'llah *and* Some Answered Questions *and I am on the way to translate a third one,* 'Abdu'l-Baha on Divine Philosophy. *For I believe in the new world order, and the eventual salvation of the world lies in the realization of the principles of Baha'u'llah and I want to perform my small part in bringing these glad tidings to our people."* In 1939, Liu completed the translation of *Prayers and Meditations* by Baha'u'llah.

During the war years from 1939 to 1945, despite the difficulties in communication, some correspondence between the Guardian and the mainland Chinese Baha'is continued. In that same period a few visiting Chinese students in America became Baha'is. One was Y. L. Chu (Chu Yao-lung) from Nanking, who became a Baha'i in Washington in April 1946. He returned to China, arriving in July 1946 and visited Mr. Husayn Uskuli, Mr. and Mrs. Suleimani, Miss Bernice Wood[118] and Mr. Jimmy Chou Chia-san[119] in Shanghai. After Chu's marriage in Shanghai on 17 August 1945, he and his wife moved to live in Nanking, arriving on 21 August. He had a government post there. He taught the Baha'i Faith to many of his friends and was able to guide his neighbour, H.C. Yuan, into the Faith.

In the period 1945 to 1949, a number of Chinese Air Force officers training in Denver, Colorado, in the United States became Baha'is after coming into contact with the Baha'is there and attending various meetings. The Chinese enquirers often visited Mrs. Elizabeth Clark and her children, who lived in Wheat Rudge outside Denver, and had informal discussions on the Baha'i

---

118 Worked in China in 1946 with United Nations Relief and Rehabilitation Administration in Shanghai. Reported that several Chinese were interested in the Baha'i Faith and that Baha'i meetings were held in Shanghai. She also reported that literature was sent to interested enquirers in Hangchow, Nanking and Hankow (see *The Baha'i World Vol XI*, p.372). Left Hong Kong on 10 August 1990 to settle in Seattle, United States.

119 Married and settled in Hawaii in 1947.

Early Chinese believers, presumably Chan S. Liu and family. Portrait hangs on the wall to the left of the entrance door into the southwest corner room of the Mansion of Bahji
(Photo courtesy of the Research Department of the Universal House of Justice)

Faith. Among those officers who accepted the Faith were Mr. David Luan Chi, Mr. Chan Tien-lee, Mr. Jimmy Chou Chia-san and Mr. M.S Yuan.[120]

---

120   Became a Baha'i in 1947 after his friends introduced him to Mrs. Mariam Haney.

Group of Chinese aviators, and other guests attending a meeting at a Baha'i International
School, July, 1945, Temerity Ranch, Colorado, United States
(The Baha'i World Vol. X p.732)

In 1949 Mr. Chu Yao-lung, Mr. Chang Tien-lee, Mr. M.S Yuan. and Mr.
H.C. Yuan moved to live in Taiwan[121] in either Taipei or Tainan, and were
probably the first Baha'is to settle in Taiwan.

Another prominent Chinese who became a Baha'i in America was Hilda Yen
Male. Hilda Yen Male (Hilda Yen Yank-Sing[122]) was born on 29 November
1905 to F.C. Yen and Siu Ying Chow, who were wealthy and prominent public
figures in Shanghai. Her family adopted the Christian Faith. At sixteen she won
an award to study at Smith College in the United States as a university cultural
exchange student, making her the youngest Chinese to have won that award.
After her graduation she returned to Shanghai and first heard of the Baha'i
Faith in 1923 through her uncle Dr. Y.S. Tsao. After her divorce she worked in
Moscow as a hostess at the Chinese embassy for her uncle, who was the
Chinese ambassador to Russia. She later moved to work in Berlin and
Switzerland. When the Manchurian war broke out in China near the beginning

---

121   Under the rule of Japan from 1895-1945.
122   *The Baha'i World Vol. XV,* p.476.

of the Second World War, she went to live in the United States. She returned to Chungking (now Chongqing), the war-time capital of China, to help with the war effort in the period 1941-43 as her father was serving as Minister of Health in the Cabinet of Chiang Kai-shek. In 1944 she returned to United States and became a Baha'i in 1945 at Wilmette, Illinois. In that same year, she worked for the Department of Public Information of the United Nations. She represented

Miss Hilda Yank Sing Yen, niece of Dr. Y.S. Tsao
(The Baha'i World Vol. XV p.476)

the Baha'is at many large public meetings in United States and Canada during her years at the United Nations and often quoted Shoghi Effendi's words in her lectures at both Baha'i and non-Baha'i meetings. In 1949 she was part of the four-member Baha'i delegation to the Third International Conference of International Non-Governmental Organizations held at Lake Success, New York, 4-9 April[123]. In 1952 she was again a member of a Baha'i delegation to the Fifth International Conference of Non-Governmental Organizations held at the United Nations Headquarters in New York, 6-10 October 1952, and served as the Vice-Chairman of the Working Committee No. 1 at the Conference[124]. Hilda Yen passed away on 18 March 1970. Hilda's long-time friend, Mildred Mottahedeh[125], wrote that the *"future history of the Baha'i Faith in China will make an enduring place for Hilda Yen* [126] *"*.

Miss Hilda Yen (third from left) as a member of the Baha'i Delegation to the United Nations International Conference of Non-Governmental Organizations, held at Lake Success, New York, April 4-9, 1949.
Left to right: Amin Banani, Mrs. Mildred R. Mottahedeh, Miss Hilda Yen, Matthew Bullock
(The Baha'i World Vol. XII p.603)

---

123 *The Baha'i World Vol. XII,* pp.601, 603.
124 *The Baha'i World Vol. XII,* pp.609-610.
125 She also served as a Baha'i Delegate to the United Nations International Conference of Non-Governmental Organizations held in New York in 1949.
126 *The Baha'i World Vol. IV,* p.431.

A New Era Begins

From 1949 until the present day, the growth of Baha'i Faith in China slowed down due mainly to the lack of religious freedom, a policy of the denial of the existence of God and the increasing suspicion of foreigners, especially Westerners, under the new Chinese Communist Party government. Since then, no active teaching of the Baha'i Faith has been carried out in mainland China. As the progress of the Baha'i Faith in China was temporarily suspended, a new and vibrant growth of the Faith was taking place in Southeast Asia and other countries of the Far East. That significant and historic period occurred prior to and during the Ten Year Teaching and Consolidation Plan, commonly known as the Ten Year World Crusade[127] (1953-1963), set in motion by Shoghi Effendi. Pioneers from all parts of the world were steadily arriving to open up the numerous virgin territories to the Cause of Baha'u'llah. Many of them were later to receive the title of Knight[128] of Baha'u'llah. As a result of the sacrifice of those early believers many countries throughout the world were opened to the Baha'i Faith.

Southeast Asia

Among the many early pioneers to arrive in Southeast Asia prior to the commencement of the Ten Year World Crusade were Dr. K.M.[129] and Mrs. Shirin[130] Fozdar. In 1950 they brought the Baha'i Faith to Singapore and Malaya, then collectively known as the Strait Settlements. Those countries were

---

127   Ten-year teaching Plan initiated by Shoghi Effendi, which commenced in 1953 and culminated in Ridvan (April) 1963. Its commencement also synchronized with the Centenary of the birth of Baha'u'llah's Mission.

128   A title initially bestowed by Shoghi Effendi upon those Baha'is who arose to open new territories to the Faith during the first years of the Ten Year Crusade and subsequently also given to those who first reached those still-unopened territories at a later date.

129   Dr. K.M. Fozdar was one of the first Indian Parsees to accept the Baha'i Faith in India (in 1925). In 1953 he pioneered to the Andaman Islands where he succeeded in confirming four people into the Baha'i Faith, and received the title of Knight of Baha'u'llah from the Guardian. He returned to Singapore after four months stay in the Andaman Islands due to the authorities refusing to allow him to prolong his stay. Dr. K.M. Fozdar passed away in 1958 in Singapore and is buried at the Baha'i Cemetery at Chuo Chu Kang (see *The Baha'i World Vol. XIII,* p.892).

130   Shirin Fozdar was born into a Baha'i family. Resident in Singapore for a long time and presently living in Bombay, India and is still actively serving the Cause.

mentioned in the Tablets of the Divine Plan[131] of 'Abdu'l-Baha. On their arrival in Singapore, in order to show the local people the Baha'i teaching of service to humanity, the Fozdars opened a free school where 300 underprivileged women were taught to read and write. The first two years were exhausting and depressing for the Fozdars due to lack of response from the local populace. Soon afterwards, however, they gradually accepted the Baha'i Faith and conditions for teaching improved when the first Local Spiritual Assembly of Singapore[132] was formed in 1952. Dr. K.M. Fozdar, Mrs. Shirin Fozdar, Dr. John Fozdar[133], Mr. Teoh Geok Leng[134] and Mr. G. Datwani[135] were some of the founding members.

Dr. K.M. and Shirin Fozdar with Martha Root (centre) in Ajmer, Rajasthan *circa* 1938
(Martha Root: Lioness at the Threshold, M.R. Garis p.454)

---

131   Fourteen Tablets revealed by 'Abdu'l-Baha during the First World War to the Baha'is of United States and Canada exhorting them to spread the Cause of Baha'u'llah to all the five continents. Some 120 countries were mentioned in the Tablet.

132   *The Baha'i World Vol. XII*, p.573.

133   Dr. Fozdar was given the title of Knight of Baha'u'llah for Brunei and is now a member of the Baha'i Continental Board of Counsellors for Asia. Mrs. Fozdar is an Auxiliary Board Member. They reside in Kuching, East Malaysia. Dr. Fozdar is the second son of Dr. K.M. and Mrs. Shirin Fozdar.

134   Passed away in 1986.

135   Accepted the Baha'i Faith in Singapore in 1952. Later settled with his wife Lachmi (who accepted the Faith in Japan in 1953) in Hong Kong on 4 August 1954.

The first Baha'i in Singapore was Mr. Naraindas, and the first public talk was probably given at the Rotary Club[136]. Mrs. George Lee[137], a prominent Chinese, was one of the early Chinese in Singapore to accept the Baha'i Faith (in February 1958[138]). She later became a member of the first National Spiritual Assembly[139] of the Baha'is of Malaysia in 1964. Perhaps the earliest Singaporean to have heard of the Baha'i Faith was a female student who heard Martha Root during a Baha'i lecture at the Hong Kong University in 1930. She was so overwhelmed with the teachings that she came to see Martha the next day and asked, "What can I do to promote the Baha'i Movement in Singapore, my home city?[140]". No information is yet available to identify that student.

Other pioneers to arrive in those regions included Dr. Rahmatu'llah Muhajir[141] and his wife[142] from Iran. Dr. R. Muhajir was born in 1923 and his family name was taken from a Tablet from 'Abdu'l-Baha bearing the salutation 'Ay Muhajiran — 'O Pioneers'. They pioneered to the Mentawai Islands, Indonesia, in 1954 thus fulfilling the wish of the Guardian. At that time the Mentawai Islands were a goal of the National Spiritual Assembly of the Baha'is of Australia and New Zealand. Dr. Rahmat and Mrs. Iran Muhajir arrived in Muara Siberut in February 1954 at the inception of the Ten Year Crusade. They were assigned to the Mentawai Islands where Dr. Muhajir worked as a medical doctor for the Indonesian Ministry of Health. Dr. and Mrs. Muhajir's dedication, constant encouragement of and love for the local believers soon brought results, with many local people becoming Baha'is and numerous Assemblies being established. When the Muhajirs left the Mentawai Islands in 1958, they had brought in more than four thousand believers, established thirty-three Local Spiritual Assemblies and a Baha'i school, purchased a Baha'i endowment land and translated a Baha'i pamphlet into the Mentawai language. Dr. Muhajir can be considered as the father of mass teaching, especially in the countries of the Philippines, India and Malaysia. He was appointed a Hand of the Cause of God in the last contingent in October 1957[143] by Shoghi Effendi. Dr. Muhajir passed away in Quito, Ecuador in October 1979.

---

136 *Per. comm.* Dr. John Fozdar.

137 Still residing in Singapore.

138 *Per. comm.* Dr. John Fozdar.

139 Nationally elected Baha'i administrative body.

140 *The Baha'i World Vol. IV,* p.432.

141 *The Baha'i World Vol. XVIII,* pp.652-659.

142 Iran Muhajir, daughter of Hand of the Cause of God, Mr. 'Ali-Akbar Furutan.

143 Shoghi Effendi appointed three contingents of Hands of the Cause of God — in December 1951, February 1952 and October 1957. Some Hands were appointed singly between March 1952 and March 1957, and some Hands were appointed posthumously.

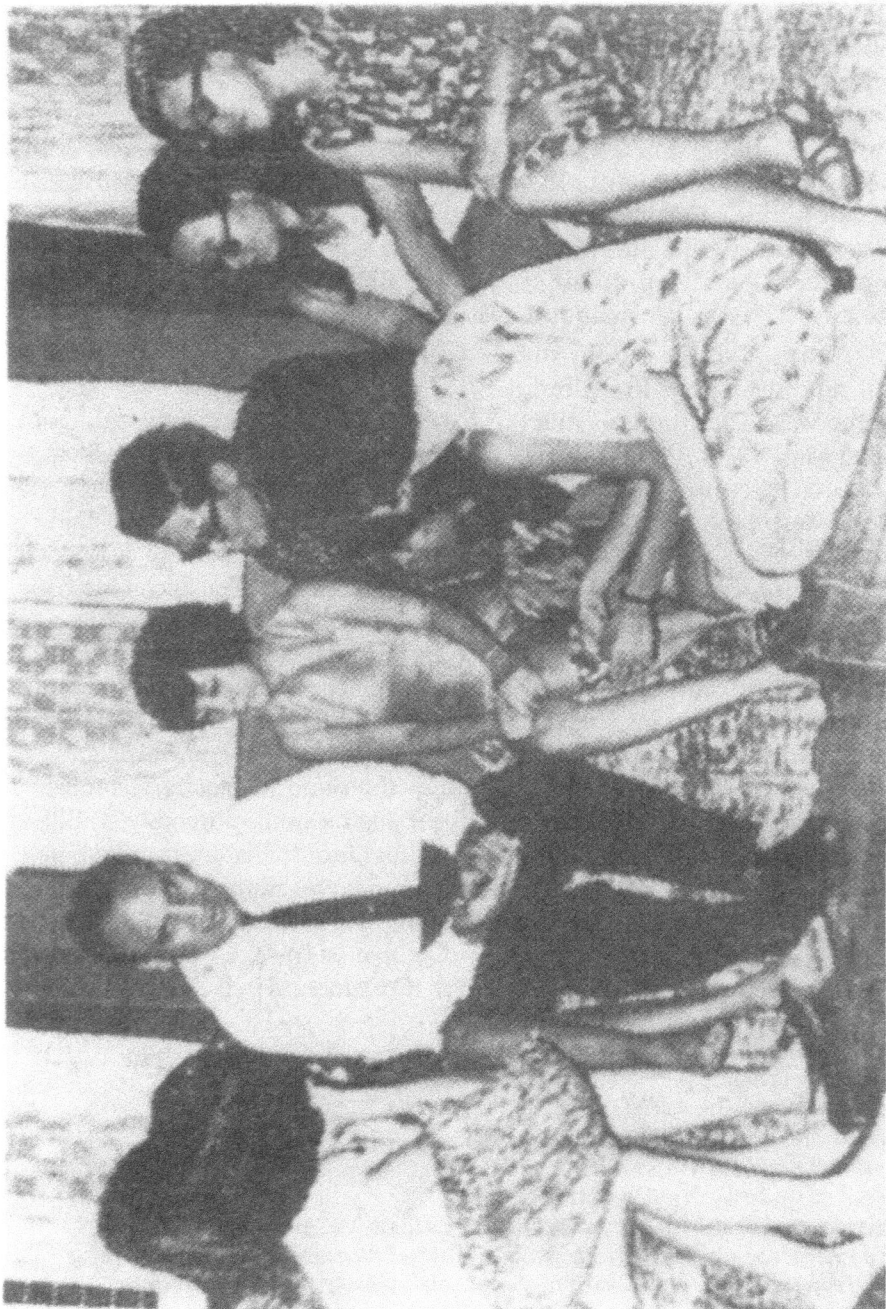

Hand of the Cause of God, Dr. Rahmatu'llah Muhajir, addressing a group of Chinese believers at the Penang Baha'i Centre, 42 Peel Avenue, Georgetown, Penang, Malaysia *circa* March 1969 (Malaysian Baha'i News Vol. 5 No. 1 p.10)

Hand of the Cause of God Dr. Rahmatu'llah Muhajir
(The Baha'i World Vol. XVIII p.652)

Other pioneers who arrived during the Ten Year Crusade to Indonesia[144] included Mr. Keykhosrow and Mrs. Parvaneh Payman[145], Dr. Manutschehr and Mrs. Malihe Gabriel[146], Mr. Aflatoon and Mrs. Talieh Payman[147], Dr. Fazullah and Mrs. Lamia Astani[148], and Dr. Nooruddin and Mrs. Bahereh Soraya[149]. Mr. Khadaram and Mrs. Parvin Payman[150] were the first pioneers in Indonesia, arriving in 1951 and had lived in India for six years.

The earliest Chinese to become a Baha'i in Indonesia was Mr. Njo Suntian in about March or April 1955 as recorded in a letter dated 13 April 1955 written by Mrs. Iran Muhajir to the Asian Teaching Committee of the National Spiritual Assembly of Baha'is of Australia and New Zealand. Mrs. Muhajir often wrote to the Committee to report the Baha'i activities in the Mentawai Islands because the islands were a teaching goal of that National Spiritual Assembly. Mr. Suntian became a Baha'i in Muara Siberut, Mentawai, Indonesia. In a letter from the Secretary of that committee to the secretary of the National Spiritual Assembly of the Baha'is of Southeast Asia dated 13 July 1957 it was recorded that two Chinese youth, Mr. Wong Ching Gea (18 years old) and Mr. Tamway (15 years old) both joined the Faith on 18 August 1956. It is probable that they could have accepted the Faith at an earlier date as Mr. Suntian's declaration was recorded as 12 December 1955 which contradicts the date of 13 April 1955 in Mrs. Muhajir's letter. There is no information currently available regarding either Mr. Suntian or the two Chinese youth. Another early Chinese to accept the Bahai Faith in Indonesia was Mrs. Lena Tan[151], who later moved to live in Singapore and later served as a member of the first National Spiritual Assembly of the Baha'is of Singapore, which was formed in 1972.

---

144   There were other families who pioneered to Indonesia during that period. It is beyond the scope of this paper to mention all of them.
145   Arrived in 1952. They moved to Melbourne, Australia in 1964. Presently pioneering in the Cook Islands.
146   Arrived on 4 June 1955. They moved to Melbourne, Australia in April 1962. Parents-in-law of the author.
147   Arrived in 1956. They moved to Melbourne, Australia in April 1966.
148   Arrived in 1954. They are still residing in Indonesia.
149   Arrived in 1954. They are still residing in Indonesia.
150   Mr. K. Payman is a former member of the Baha'i Continental Board of Counsellors for Asia. He and his wife are still residing in Jakarta. Khadaram, Aflatoon and Keykhosrow Payman are brothers.
151   Presently residing in Singapore.

Mr. Harry Clarke[152], Mr. Charles Duncan[153], Dr. John and Mrs. Greta Fozdar, and Mr. Minoo and Mrs. Marjorie Fozdar[154] pioneered to Brunei. Mr. Jamshed Fozdar[155] pioneered to Vietnam. Mr. Hismatullah Azizi[156] pioneered to mainland China and later to Macau. Mr. Udai Narain Singh[157] pioneered to Sikkim in 1953 and later to Tibet in 1956. Jeanne Frankel[158] and her mother, Mrs. Margaret Bates[159], pioneered to Nicobar Islands[160] in 1957, and were in Kota Kinabalu, Sabah, for three months[161] before returning to the United States. There were also many others who arrived as pioneers in those regions.

It was through the untiring effort and vision of Mr. Yan Kee Leong[162], described by the Universal House of Justice as the first enlightened Baha'i of Malaysia[163], who further expanded the progress of the Baha'i Faith, especially among the Chinese in those regions. Yan Kee Leong first heard of the Faith in 1949 at the Pan-Pacific Peace Conference in India and became the first believer in the Federation of Malaya (West Malaysia[164]) on 19 December 1953[165] at the age of 54. At that time there were Baha'is in Kuching[166], Sarawak (now part of East Malaysia), which was then a British Colony. They were Stephen Wong, Jimmy Sim, Tan Teck Kee, and Mr. and Mrs. C.K. Chih, and were members

---

152 Knight of Baha'u'llah for Brunei. Arrived in Brunei in 1954.
153 Knight of Baha'u'llah for Brunei. He pioneered to Brunei in 1954 and later to Macau. He now resides in Okinawa.
154 Mr. Fozdar is an Auxiliary Board Member and the youngest son of Dr. K.M. and Mrs. Shirin Fozdar. Mr. and Mrs. Fozdar now reside in Geraldton, Western Australia.
155 Eldest son of Dr. K.M. and Mrs. Shirin Fozdar. He and his wife now reside in Singapore.
156 Arrived in Hong Kong on 8 March 1954 and left in 1985 to live in Canada.
157 Knight of Baha'u'llah for Sikkim and Tibet (see *The Baha'i World Vol.XIII*, p.455).
158 Knight of Baha'u'llah for Nicobar Islands (see *The Baha'i World Vol.XIII*, p.454).
159 Knight of Baha'u'llah for Nicobar Islands (see *The Baha'i World Vol.XIII*, p.454).
160 Located in the Andaman Sea and north of Sumatra.
161 *Per. comm.* Dr. John Fozdar.
162 For an account of his early life see Henry Ong. *Uncle Yankee.* Ong Publication, California, U.S.A., 1979. Henry Ong is a grandson of Yan Kee Leong.
163 Letter from Counsellor Dr. John Fozdar to Singapore 19 Day Feast Newsletter dated 23 November 1986.
164 Malaysia was formed on 16 September 1963 amalgamating Malaya, Sarawak and British North Borneo (Sabah).
165 *Singapore 19 Day Feast Newsletter* 1 August 1986.
166 *Per. comm.* Dr. John Fozdar.

of the first Local Spiritual Assembly of Kuching formed in 1953[167] Yan Kee Leong was born in Selangor, Malaysia, on 19 November 1899, the son of a tin-miner. He converted to the Catholic Faith and worked as a chemist and dispenser, and as an artist and cartoonist for local newspapers. He taught the Baha'i Faith to many of his theosophist friends in Seremban, Malaysia, resulting in some of them becoming Baha'is. As a result the first Local Spiritual Assembly of the Baha'is of Seremban was formed on 21 April 1954. Uncle Yankee, as he is lovingly called by the believers in the region, was a 'spiritual father' to many Baha'is in Malaysia and the surrounding countries. He travelled extensively, promoting the Baha'i Faith and actively teaching the Chinese people in the region, bringing in the first Chinese believers in Burma[168] and the Philippines[169]. He was elected to the first National Spiritual Assembly of the Baha'is of Malaysia in 1964 and elected secretary. He was appointed to the Continental Board of Counsellors[170] for the South East Asian Zone in 1968. Uncle Yankee passed away in Ipoh, Malaysia, on 17 June 1986, at the age of

Mr. Yan Kee Leong (centre) with the first two Chinese to accept the Faith in Burma
(The Baha'i World Vol. XV p.253)

---

167   *The Baha'i World Vol. XII*, p.573.
168   *The Baha'i World Vol. XV*, p.253.
169   *The Baha'i World Vol. XV*, p.253.
170   Continental Baha'i administrative institution responsible for protection and promulgation of the Baha'i Faith. It was formed in June 1968.

eighty-six, after thirty-two years of active service to the Faith of Baha'u'llah. In a condolence cable to the Malaysian Baha'i community, the Universal House of Justice stated that Yan Kee Leong *"inspired His loving followers and set example for the friends belonging to the great Chinese race by raising foundation divine civilization on earth"*[171].

Leong Tat Chee, an early Chinese believer in Malaysia
(The Baha'i World Vol. XV, p.527)

Another Chinese believer who contributed significantly to the progress of the Baha'i Faith in those regions was Mr. Leong Tat Chee[172]. He became a Baha'i in 1955 after hearing about the Faith through Dr. and Mrs. K.M. Fozdar in Malacca, Malaysia. Prior to his acceptance of the Baha'i Faith, Leong Tat Chee was an official of a society which comprised a federation of five religions — Taoism, Confucianism, Buddhism, Christianity and Islam, the major faiths of the region. He was elected Chairman of the first Local Spiritual Assembly of Malacca, Malaysia, formed in 1955. He donated his house to the National Spiritual Assembly of the Baha'is of Malaysia to become the Baha'i Centre of

171 *Singapore 19 Day Feast Newsletter* 1 August 1986
172 *The Baha'i World Vol. XV,* p.527.

Malacca and had the honour of representing the Chinese race at the World Congress[173] held in London in 1963. In 1964 Leong Tat Chee was elected to the first National Spiritual Assembly of the Baha'is of Malaysia and in the same year was also appointed to the Auxiliary Board[174]. In 1965 accompanied by' Mr. Yan Kee Leong, he went on an extended Chinese teaching trip to Hong Kong, Macau and Taiwan. He was also instrumental in enlightening the Malaysian believers regarding the importance of Chinese teaching and the significance of China awakening to the Faith in the future.

Mr. Hushmand Fatheazam (standing), member of the Universal House of Justice, addressing a large gathering of Chinese Baha'is and enquirers in Taiping, Malaysia. Mr. Leong Tat Chee (seated left) with Chairman and Secretary of Local Spiritual Assembly of Taiping *circa* September 1965
(Malaysian Baha'i News Vol. 1 No. 2 p.23)

---

173   Centenary of the declaration of Baha'u'llah in Baghdad.
174   Baha'i Administrative institution first formed in 1954. Initially it had the duty of assisting the Hands of the Cause of God. It came under the direction of the Continental Board of Counsellors after its inception.

First Spiritual Assembly of the Bahá'ís of Singapore, 1952 Standing (left to right): Mr. Toh Beng Wang, Mr. Kishinchand, Dr. John Fozdar, Mr. Motiram Seated (left to right): Mr. Teoh Geok Leng, Mr. Gianchand B. Datwani, Mrs. Shirin Fozdar, Dr. K.M. Fozdar, Mr. Ramsay
(The Bahá'í World Vol. XII p.573)

First Spiritual Assembly of the Baha'is of Kuching, Sarawak, East Malaysia, 1953
(The Baha'i World Vol. XII p.578)

First Spiritual Assembly of the Baha'is of Victoria, Hong Kong, 1956 Standing (left to right): Mr. Anthony Seto, Mr. Gianchand B. Datwani, Mr. Paul Shia, Mr. Hismatullah Azizi Seated (left to right): Mr. Chan Lie Fan, Mrs. Mamie Loretta Seto, Mrs. Mary Shia, Mr. Chan Lie Kun.
(The Baha'i World Vol. XIII p.1132)

First Spiritual Assembly of the Bahá'ís of Brunei Town, Brunei, 1957 Seated (left to right): Mr. Shaik Muhammad, Mr. Cheah Teck Heng, Mr. Minoo Fozdar, Miss Kong Siew Yin, Mr. Cheok (first Bahá'í in Brunei), Mr. Chin Yun Sang. Standing (left to right): Mr. Robert Cheok, Mr. Ratilal Tribhuran, Mr. Sia (The Bahá'í World Vol. XIII p.1150)

First Spiritual Assembly of the Baha'is of Taipei, Taiwan, 1958
(The Baha'i World Vol. XIII p.1081)

First Spiritual Assembly of the Baha'is of Phnom Penh, Cambodia, April 1959. Mr. Chester Lee is standing second from the left. (The Baha'i World Vol. XIII p.1038)

The Far East

On 20 October 1953 Mrs. Francis Heller[175] arrived as a pioneer in Macau from the United States and remained there till 4 November 1954 when she returned home. She was the first Baha'i known to have lived in Macau. On 8 December 1953 Mr. Carl Scherer[176] and his wife, Loretta, arrived from the United States to settle in Macau, remaining there till 6 January 1959. All three early pioneers were to receive the title of Knight of Baha'u'llah for that region. The first resident Chinese in Macau, Mr. Harry Yim[177], accepted the Baha'i Faith on 15 July 1954. The first Spiritual Assembly of Macau was formed in 1958, but only in 1989 was the first National Spiritual Assembly of the Baha'is of Macau formed, the Hand of the Cause of God 'Amatu'l-Baha Ruhiyyih Khanum[178] representing the Universal House of Justice on that occasion.

Carl A. (left) and Loretta L. Scherer, Knights of Baha'u'llah for Macau
(The Baha'i World Vol. XVIII p.738)

---

175   *The Baha'i World Vol. XIII,* p.449, XVIII, p.738-740. She passed away in 1990.
176   The Scherers lived in China from 1931-1936 as Carl was working for Texas Oil Co.
177   Harry Yim is still living in Macau.
178   Born Mary Sutherland Maxwell. Wife of Shoghi Effendi. Appointed Hand of the Cause of God in 1952.

Baha'i of Macau, 14 June 1955
Seated (left to right): Manuel Ferreira, Mary Tung (Mrs. P. Shia), Loretta Scherer, Paul Kao
(young boy Louis Shia)
Standing (left to right): Paul Shia, John Z.T. Chang, Carl Scherer, Harry Yim, William Yang
(Photo courtesy of the Research Department of the Universal House of Justice)

Other Baha'is who arrived to settle in that region included Mr. and Mrs. Gian Datwani, who arrived in Hong Kong on 4 August 1954, and Mr. and Mrs. Anthony Seto, who arrived in Hong Kong from San Francisco in the autumn of the same year as Ten Year Crusade pioneers. The Setos had ample opportunity to proclaim the Baha'i Faith to many prominent Chinese, Indian and English residents in Hong Kong, due mainly to Mrs. Seto being the Social Secretary of the United Nations Association. In 1956 they had to return to the United States as Mr. Seto required medical treatment. He passed away in Tokyo in 1957 due to ill health while on his way back to Hong Kong and he is buried at the International Cemetery in Yokohama. Mrs. Seto remained in Hong Kong till 1963 although, due to her poor health, she had the choice of completing her Ten Year Crusade pioneering commitment in the more temperate climate of New Zealand. She left Hong Kong to settle in Burlingame,

California. On 12 February 1956 four individuals accepted the Baha'i Faith in Hong Kong, becoming the first Baha'is in the Colony. They were Mr. Nari Sherwani[179], Mr. Ng Ying Kay, Mr. Chan Lie Kun and his twin brother Mr. Chan Lie Fun. The first Local Spiritual Assembly in Hong Kong was formed in 1956.

In October 1953 Hand of the Cause of God, Mr. Zikrullah Khadem, visited Taiwan, during which time three Chinese, Professor L.S. Tsao, Mr. Jimmy Hong Li-ming and Mr. Wong He-len, accepted the Baha'i Faith at a meeting at the home of Mr. Chu Yao-lung. By that time more Chinese were becoming Baha'is. In 1955 Mr. Ho Cheng-tsu, Mr. C.C. Cheng, Mr. C.C. Pai and Mr. Johnson Siao became Baha'is in Taiwan through the teaching effort of the Suleimanis. The first All-Taiwan Teaching Conference was held in Tainan in November 1956. It was hosted by the Suleimanis and attended by Agnes Alexander and forty other Baha'is. The first Summer School in Taiwan was also held in Tainan a few months later. Hand of the Cause of God Mr. Jalal Khazeh visited Taiwan in July that same year.

In August 1958 a Baha'i in Macau, Mr. Cheong Siu Choi (also known as John Z.T. Chang[180]), together with his wife Margaret and son Jackson, visited Hainan Island situated off the coast of mainland China close to the North Vietnamese border. Due to the political atmosphere on the island, the Hainanese were not interested in accepting the Bahai Faith. The Guardian awarded the title of Knight of Baha'u'llah for Hainan Island to Mr. Z.T. Chang..

The 'Talented Race'

As a result of the pioneering efforts and self sacrifice of the early believers during the Ten Year World Crusade, Baha'i communities were gradually established throughout the region. Many of those early believers who accepted the Faith of Baha'u'llah were Chinese. By the 1950s many Baha'i Local Spiritual Assemblies and communities had been established. At the beginning of the Ten Year Crusade in Southeast Asia, only three Local Spiritual Assemblies were established, namely, in Singapore, Kuching and Solano (Philippines), and a total of not more then ten localities had Baha'i residents[181].

---

179   Now living in Ireland. Often visits Hong Kong.
180   *The Baha'i World Vol. XIII, p.449, XVIII*, p.738-740.
181   *The Baha'i World Vol. XIII*, pp.301-304.

The first Local Spiritual Assembly of Singapore was formed in 1952, and the first Local Spiritual Assembly of British Borneo (now Sarawak, East Malaysia) was formed in Kuching in 1953. By 1956 thirteen Assemblies had been formed — five in Indonesia, four in Malaya (now West Malaysia), two in the Philippines and one each in Sarawak and Vietnam. The first Local Spiritual Assembly of Jakarta was formed in 1954. In 1956, the first Local Spiritual Assemblies of Kwangju in Korea, Victoria in Hong Kong and Tainan in Taiwan were formed respectively. In 1957 the first Local Spiritual Assembly of Brunei Town in Brunei was formed. In 1958 the first Spiritual Assembly of Macau was formed and the first Taiwan Baha'i Centre was established in Tainan. In September 1958 the last of the Intercontinental Baha'i Conferences called by the Guardian was to be held in Jakarta but it had to be transferred to Singapore because the permit for its holding was withheld just a week before it was due to convene. Hand of the Cause of God and Secretary of the International Baha'i Council[182], Mr. Leroy Ioas, was the representative of the Guardian at the Conference. Some of the significant events at that gathering included the viewing of the portrait of Baha'u'llah, and the news of the enrolment of many Chinese Baha'is from Sarawak and Brunei, as well as Filipinos, Japanese, Laotians and Cambodians — members of both the brown and yellow races. In 1959 the first Local Spiritual Assembly of Phnom Penh in Cambodia was formed. Most of the early believers in Indo-China were Indo-Chinese and not Chinese[183]. Mr. Chester Lee[184] was one of the few Chinese to accept the Baha'i Faith in Cambodia, and was a member of the first Local Spiritual Assembly of Phnom Penh and the first National Spiritual Assembly of the Baha'is of Hong Kong. In Southeast Asia at the end of the Ten Year World Crusade, there were well over 750 Baha'i centres, of which over half had established Local Spiritual Assemblies.

By that stage many Chinese in the region were becoming Baha'is, especially in Malaysia. The first Teaching Conference in Chinese in that country was held in Ipoh in 1966[185]. It was attended by many of the early Chinese believers like Mr. Huang Chern Sing, Mr. Loh Theam Seang, Mr. Woo (Chairman of Local

---

182   *"The first embryonic (Baha'i) International Institution"*, appointed by Shoghi Effendi on 9
       January 1951.
183   *Per. comm.* Dr. John Fozdar.
184   Moved to live in Hong Kong in the early 1970s. Was a former member of the Baha'i
       International Community Committee for China.
185   *Malaysian Baha'i News Vol. 2 No. 2.* Publisher National Spiritual Assembly of the Baha'is of
       Malaysia, pp.13-14.

Spiritual Assembly of Taiping), Mrs. Teresa Chee[186] and Mr. Yeoh Chai Lye. Those teaching activities consequently resulted in the establishment of many more Baha'i localities and Local Spiritual Assemblies, culminating in the establishment of many strong National Spiritual Assemblies in the region, such as the formation of the first National Spiritual Assembly of the Baha'is of Malaysia in 1964, the Hand of the Cause of God 'Amatu'l-Baha Ruhiyyih Khanum representing the Universal House of Justice on that occasion. In 1967 the first National Spiritual Assembly of Taiwan was elected. By 1971 five Assemblies had been formed in Singapore and in the following year the first National Spiritual Assembly of the Baha'is of Singapore was elected, Hand of the Cause Mr. Jalal Khazeh representing the Universal House of Justice. The first National Spiritual Assembly of Hong Kong was elected in 1974, Amatu'l-Baha Ruhiyyih Khanum representing the Universal House of Justice on that occasion.

The first National Spiritual Assembly of the Baha'is of Malaysia formed in Ridvan 1964.
Seated (left to right): Mrs. Greta Fozdar, Hand of the Cause of God 'Amatu'l-Baha Ruhiyyih Khanum (representative of the Universal House of Justice), Mrs. George Lee, Mrs. Marjorie Fozdar.
Standing (left to right): Mr. Yan Kee Leong, Mr. Harlan Lang, Mr. John Fozdar, Mr. Leong Tat Chee, Mr. Minoo Fozdar, Mr. Chin Yun Sang.
(The Baha'i World Vol. XIV p.522)

---

186   Daughter of Yan Kee Leong and now an Auxiliary Board Member.

The first National Spiritual Assembly of the Baha'is of Brunei formed in Ridvan 1966. Hand of the Cause of God Collis Featherstone (representative of the Universal House of Justice, seated sixth from the left)
(The Baha'i World Vol. XIV p.534)

The first National Spiritual Assembly of the Baha'is of Taiwan formed in Ridvan 1967 (one member missing)
Standing (left to right) Kuo Rong-hui, Robert Yen chih-Hsiung, Dr. S.I. Dean, S.A. Suleimani, Tsao Kai-min, Huang Tzen-min. Seated (left to right) Isabelle Dean, Riduani Suleimani
(The Baha'i World Vol. XIV p.542)

The first National Spiritual Assembly of the Baha'is of Hong Kong formed in Ridvan 1974. Seated (left to right): Counsellor Mr. Khudarahm Payman, Hand of the Cause of God 'Amatu'l-Baha Ruhiyyih Khanum (representative of the Universal House of Justice), Counsellor Mr. Yan Kee Leong, Mrs. Lachmi Datwani. Standing (left to right): Mr. Chester Lee, Mr. Hismatullah Azizi, Mr. Charles Duncan, Mr. Attar, Mr. Gian Datwani, Mr. Lawrence Ip, Mr. David Hockson, Mr. Tom Lane.
(The Baha'i World Vol. XVI p.452)

The first National Spiritual Assembly of the Baha'is of Singapore formed in Ridvan 1972.
Seated (left to right): Mrs. Shirin Fozdar, Counsellor Mr. Khudarahm Payman, Hand of the
Cause of God Jalal Khazeh (representative of the Universal House of Justice), Counsellors
Mr. Yan Kee Leong and Dr. Chellie Sundram.
Standing (left to right): Mr. Kenneth Mak, Mrs. Lena Tan, Mrs. George Lee, Mrs. Rose
Ong, Mr. Teoh Geok Leng, Mr. Machamboo, Mr. Edward Teo, Miss Nita Sundram, Mr.
Henry Ong
(The Baha'i World Vol. XV p.157)

It was at the historic Oceanic Conference held at the Victoria Memorial Hall
in Singapore in January 1971 that the importance of teaching the Chinese race
was emphasised for the first time by the Universal House of Justice. In its
message to that Conference, they stated *"..a number of Chinese-speaking believers
must arise who, as pioneers and travelling teachers in all the countries of South East
Asia, will attract large numbers of the talented Chinese race to embrace and serve
the Faith of Baha'u'llah."* The spiritual destiny of the Chinese people was now
determined and the teaching direction put into motion. Ever since that historic
conference, Chinese teaching has become more dynamic and visionary,
resulting in the enrolment of many Chinese believers throughout the region.
Chinese teaching is now being carried out intensively in many countries,
especially in Southeast Asia, the Far East and Australia.

China — the Last Frontier

But the stage for reaching the majority of the Chinese people in China was
still not set until the Universal House of Justice, on 25 June 1989, in a

momentous message stated: *"In pursuance of steps already taken for the promotion for the Faith in China, the Universal House of Justice has concluded that it is timely for the knowledge of the Baha'i Faith to be disseminated on the mainland of China as widely and as quickly as circumstances and the interest of the Chinese themselves will allow"*. At long last the Faith of Baha'u'llah could once again be heard on Chinese soil, home of one-quarter of humanity's population. In an earlier message dated 19 April 1989, the Universal House of Justice emphasised that *"...As Baha'is, we have been entrusted with the responsibility of taking the message of Baha'u'llah to all mankind, but only a comparatively small beginning has yet been made to take the teachings to the vast population of China. The Universal House of Justice feels that this task must be regarded as one of the highest priorities for the entire Baha'i world."*

Bibliography

H.D. Baker. *Chinese Family and Kinship.* MacMillan Press, London, 1979.

H.M. Balyuzi. *Baha'u'llah, the King of Glory.* George Ronald, Oxford, 1980.

H.M. Balyuzi. *Eminent Baha'is in the time of Baha'u'llah.* George Ronald, Oxford, 1985.

M.R. Garis. *Martha Root: Lioness at the Threshold.* Baha'i Publishing Trust, Wilmette, Illinois, 1983.

Malaysian Baha'i News. Publisher National Spiritual Assembly of the Baha'is of Malaysia.

Milton Osborne. *Southeast Asia: An Illustrated Introductory History.* Allen & Unwin, Sydney, 1988.

Research Department of the Universal House of Justice Notes on the Chronology of Baha'is in China, Baha'i World Centre 1986 and 9 March 1990.

Mona Gabriel-Seow. *Spiritual Realities In Traditional Chinese Beliefs And The Similarities To The Baha'i Faith.* Paper presented at the Association for Baha'i Studies Australia National Conference, Perth, Western Australia, 1989.

Jimmy Seow. *Chinese Culture and Teaching The Baha'i Faith.* Proceedings of the Baha'i Studies Conference 1987. Published by the Association for Baha'i Studies (Australian Committee), pp.1-11.

Shoghi Effendi. *God Passes By.* Baha'i Publishing Trust, Wilmette, Illinois, 1970.

Star of the West Vol. 13, 21. George Ronald, Oxford, 1984.

Jonathan D. Spence. *The Gate of Heavenly Peace: The Chinese and Their Revolution 1895-1980.* Penguin Books, U.K., 1982.

The Baha'i World Vol. II-XV, XVII, XVIII. Baha'i Publishing Trust, Wilmette, Illinois.

Witold Rodzinski. *The Walled Kingdom: A History of China from 2000 BC to the Present.* Fontana Paperbacks, London, 1984.

Biographical Notes

Jimmy E.H. Seow was born in Georgetown, Penang, Malaysia, of Chinese ancestry in 1954. He comes from a Chinese Buddhist background and accepted the Baha'i Faith in Penang in 1970. In 1975 and 1976 he studied at the University of Malaya, Kuala Lumpur, Malaysia before transferring to the University of Waikato, Hamilton, New Zealand in 1977 where he obtained a BSc. and MSc. (Hons) degree in Earth Sciences. In 1981 he returned to Malaysia and then worked as geophysical consultant in Singapore. He migrated to Australia in 1983, where he worked as a geologist. Currently he is working as a Senior Environmental Officer with the Petroleum Division, Department of Mines Western Australia and is a PhD Research Fellow with the Department of Plant Nutrition and Soil Sciences of the University of Western Australia, Perth. His doctoral thesis is in the field of soil science, geomorphology and surface hydrology. Jimmy Seow has served on numerous Baha'i committees, both national and local, in various countries and has given talks on various aspects of the Faith in Asia, Australia, New Zealand and the Pacific. He is also the author of *Study Guide for the Dawn-breakers* (Baha'i Publishing Trust of Malaysia, 1982). Jimmy Seow is now serving as an Assistant for Chinese Teaching to the Auxiliary Board Member for Propagation for Western Australia, a member of the Local Spiritual Assembly of the Baha'is of the City of Cockburn, and of the Baha'i Institute for Chinese Teaching. He is married to a Baha'i, Mona Gabriel-Seow, and has one child, Layli.

The author Jimmy Seow, his wife Mona Gabriel-Seow and daughter Layli

NOTES

NOTES

NOTES

www.ingramcontent.com/pod-product-compliance
Lightning Source LLC
Chambersburg PA
CBHW060410050426

42449CB00009B/1944